PHILOSOPHY, ANIMALITY
AND THE LIFE SCIENCES

Crosscurrents

Exploring the development of European thought through engagements with the arts, humanities, social sciences and sciences

Series Editor
Christopher Watkin, University of Cambridge

Editorial Advisory Board

Andrew Benjamin
Martin Crowley
Simon Critchley
Frederiek Depoortere
Oliver Feltham
Patrick ffrench
Christopher Fynsk
Kevin Hart
Emma Wilson

Titles available in the series:

Difficult Atheism: Post-Theological Thinking in Alain Badiou, Jean-Luc Nancy and Quentin Meillassoux
by Christopher Watkin

Politics of the Gift: Exchanges in Poststructuralism
by Gerald Moore

Unfinished Worlds: Hermeneutics, Aesthetics and Gadamer
by Nicholas Davey

The Figure of This World: Agamben and the Question of Political Ontology
by Mathew Abbott

The Becoming of the Body: Contemporary Women's Writing in French
by Amaleena Damlé

Philosophy, Animality and the Life Sciences
by Wahida Khandker

Forthcoming Titles:

Sublime Art: Towards an Aesthetics of the Future
by Stephen Zepke

The Event Universe: The Revisionary Metaphysics of Alfred North Whitehead
by Leemon McHenry

Visit the Crosscurrents website at www.euppublishing.com/series/cross

PHILOSOPHY, ANIMALITY AND THE LIFE SCIENCES

Wahida Khandker

EDINBURGH
University Press

Edinburgh University Press Ltd
The Tun – Holyrood Road
12 (2f) Jackson's Entry
Edinburgh EH8 8PJ
www.euppublishing.com

Typeset in 10.5/13 Sabon by
Servis Filmsetting Ltd, Stockport, Cheshire,
and printed and bound in Great Britain by
CPI Group (UK) Ltd, Croydon CR0 4YY

A CIP record for this book is available from the British Library

ISBN 978 0 7486 7677 4 (hardback)
ISBN 978 0 7486 7678 1 (webready PDF)

Contents

Acknowledgements

I am grateful to Carol Macdonald at Edinburgh University Press, for encouraging me to develop this project, and the Series Editor, Christopher Watkin, for reading and extensively commenting upon an early version of the manuscript. I also owe a debt of gratitude to the following: my colleagues at Manchester Metropolitan University, Ann Clarke, John Mullarkey, and all of the animal advocates I have met along the way, whose commitment and compassion have inspired this book.

Series Editor's Preface

Two or more currents flowing into or through each other create a turbulent crosscurrent, more powerful than its contributory flows and irreducible to them. Time and again, modern European thought creates and exploits crosscurrents in thinking, remaking itself as it flows through, across and against discourses as diverse as mathematics and film, sociology and biology, theology, literature and politics. The work of Gilles Deleuze, Jacques Derrida, Slavoj Žižek, Alain Badiou, Bernard Stiegler and Jean-Luc Nancy, among others, participates in this fundamental remaking. In each case disciplines and discursive formations are engaged, not with the aim of performing a pre-determined mode of analysis yielding a 'philosophy of x', but through encounters in which thought itself can be transformed. Furthermore, these fundamental transformations do not merely seek to account for singular events in different sites of discursive or artistic production but rather to engage human existence and society as such, and as a whole. The cross-disciplinarity of this thought is therefore neither a fashion nor a prosthesis; it is simply part of what 'thought' means in this tradition.

Crosscurrents begins from the twin convictions that this re-making is integral to the legacy and potency of European thought, and that the future of thought in this tradition must defend and develop this legacy in the teeth of an academy that separates and controls the currents that flow within and through it. With this in view, the series provides an exceptional site for bold, original and opinion-changing monographs that actively engage European thought in this fundamentally cross-disciplinary manner, riding existing crosscurrents and creating new ones. Each book in the series explores the different ways in which European thought develops through its engagement with disciplines across the arts, humanities, social sciences and sciences, recognising that the community of scholars working with this thought is itself spread across diverse faculties. The object of the series is therefore nothing less than to examine and carry forward the unique legacy of European thought as an inherently and irreducibly cross-disciplinary enterprise.

Christopher Watkin

Introduction

At the eastern edge of Hyde Park in London stands the Animals in War Memorial, opened in 2004 to help mark the 90th anniversary of the commencement of the First World War. An inscription marks its purpose: 'This monument is dedicated to all the animals that served and died alongside British and Allied forces in wars and campaigns throughout time.'[1] It is true that such an effort to memorialise animal lives lost helps to throw light upon the often unacknowledged use of animal labour in warfare over the centuries. However, an additional inscription is telling. It simply says, 'They had no choice.' This is both a quiet acknowledgement of the status of domestic animals in all aspects of their servility to human beings, but also a seemingly unwitting statement of an age-long characterisation of animals, in opposition to human beings, as devoid of reason and the ability to make choices.

If the monument successfully opens up questions and debates about our use of animals such as horses, dogs and pigeons in the context of warfare, it perhaps also risks obscuring the fact of the continued use of such animals, and numerous other species, in weapons testing, as well as more widely for scientific research of various kinds. For example, in 2012, the campaigning organisation the British Union for the Abolition of Vivisection reported on a range of experiments carried out at a military research laboratory in the UK, including the use of live pigs to study the effects of explosive blasts on the body. Live pigs were also used to test the effects of poisonous agents such as sulphur mustard and anthrax.[2] In the face of such experiments, then, does the presence of the war monument give a false impression of progress in our attitudes towards the uses and abuses of other animals?

One might ask the same question about the 'three Rs' principles for animal research: replacement, reduction, refinement. These principles seem to acknowledge that animal experimentation is undesirable, at least due to its basic conflict with animal interests and welfare. But the underlying assumption beneath this refrain is that ultimately animal experimentation is necessary. It could be said that this duality between the memorialised and the experimented upon describes the impasse reached in debates on animal ethics that are based on the discourse of rights. A number of commentators in the growing field of 'Critical Animal Studies' have responded to this impasse by, for example, suggesting a shift in focus from the capacities or identities of other animals (whether they can reason, speak, or suffer) towards the complex formations of inter-species relationships that define humans and animals alike.[3] Thus, in addition to Jeremy Bentham's move to place the capacity to suffer at the centre of ethical debate, the possibility arises for a more profound consideration of the problem of suffering as an irruption in rational subjective identity. Suffering, then, marks

> the limits of that subject – that subject as it is opened to others, whether it likes it or not. It is not the kind of ability animal welfare advocates cite in order to prove that animals are like us and therefore deserve rights like us. It is not an ability or capacity that we possess or control. Rather, we are possessed by it. Embodied vulnerability, then, is not only what we share with animals; it is also what limits our own sovereignty and autonomy. It is the limit of the human in the face of the animal.[4]

This move towards a thinking of the animal as 'a limit case for theories of difference, otherness, and power' is also one, it has been argued, that characterises the 'coming of age' of animal studies as a discipline in its own right.[5]

THE CONCEPT OF 'PATHOLOGICAL LIFE'

The means for understanding such shifts in our treatment of non-human animal species, as well as the human/animal distinction itself, is suggested in Michel Foucault's Introduction to the defining work of Georges Canguilhem, *The Normal and the Pathological*:

> We understand why Canguilhem's thought, his work as a historian and philosopher, could have so decisive an importance in France for all those who, starting from different points of view (whether the theorists of Marxism, psychoanalysis or linguistics), have tried to rethink the question of the subject. Phenomenology could indeed introduce the body, sexuality, death, the perceived world into the field of analysis; the Cogito remained central; neither the rationality of science nor the specificity of the life sciences could compromise its founding role. It is to this philosophy of meaning, subject and the experienced thing that Canguilhem has opposed a philosophy of error, concept and the living thing.[6]

Describing not only the significant impact of Canguilhem's writings on French thought, not least on Foucault himself, this is first a statement of the dominance of the Cogito in the history of philosophy and the centrality of the subject-object relation in determining our understanding of consciousness and life. Foucault then identifies the possibilities for rethinking relation through the counter-movements of negativity and otherness. This is not to forget the efforts of post-phenomenological thinkers such as Levinas, Sartre and Merleau-Ponty, all of whom bring questions of the 'negativity of life' (that is, life understood in terms other than the capacity to think or reason) to the fore (in alterity, nothingness and embodiment). It is, rather, to acknowledge the depth of Canguilhem's engagements with the life sciences and how the emergence of an alternative boundary between the normal and the pathological in particular has effected a new, and continually developing, analysis of the living organism against the grain of traditional taxonomical hierarchies, as well as the physical sciences.

I want to suggest that a commencement in our rethinking of animality occurs in two simple claims made in *The Normal and the Pathological*. The first concerns the object of Canguilhem's critique which is directed against the view that the relation between normal and pathological states is one of degree, or that pathology is merely a quantitative increase in the characteristics of the organism in its normal state (for example, diseased states would be described with the prefixes of *hyper-* or *hypo-*).[7] Medical enquiry would come to adopt a concept of the pathological state of the body that both signifies the redundancy of positive concepts of life (force, or animating principle) and the importance of the study of disease in the advancement of the knowledge of life: 'We think that health is life in the silence of the organs, that consequently the biologically normal . . . is revealed only through infraction of the norm and that concrete or scientific awareness of life exists only through disease.'[8] Such a view, it seems, would also come to encapsulate the value that is placed on the artificial inducement of pathological states in animals for the purposes of research into disease.

The second claim concerns the universality or application of pathological categories as principles for the understanding, where it is rather the case that measures of normality and pathology are imprecise when several individuals are considered at once, but serve as reasonably precise terms when applied to one individual considered successively over time.[9] The category of the pathological would thus acquire the somewhat contradictory status of negative indicator of the optimal conditions of organic functioning, but one that must be 'recalibrated' to account for the vital functions of each organism considered, such is the potential for variation across individuals.

We have here, in this briefest of glimpses into the development of the category of the pathological, an expression of the movement from the vital to the mortal (negative, exceptional) concepts of the organism, and the need for medicine to become an 'art of living' in recognition of the specificity of pathogenesis in each individual patient. What Canguilhem will call the 'devitalisation of life' on the one hand, and the theorisation of the specificity of biological processes, even down to the level of individuals, on the other, will be two key tendencies that I will trace in the course of this work. There is no single factor that has influenced prevailing attitudes towards the status of other animals as our inferiors (intellectually, morally, and in evolutionary terms), and the justifications for their use in scientific research. Nevertheless, some insights into this subordination of animal life can, of course, be gained from an examination of the array of cultural, political, philosophical and scientific concepts underpinning the policies and methodological ideals that determine the contemporary practices of scientists, whether in the context of privately or state-funded laboratories or in higher education institutions. In this book, the aim is to undertake an analysis of certain tendencies in the development of the ideas of animal and organic life that have helped to increase the sense of distance between human and non-human animals. This is the case, for example, in the reduction of life to a set of functions expressible in terms of the genome, but also, as Foucault suggests of Canguilhem's work, in a countermovement (of concepts of error and unpredictability) that indicates the irreducibility of life to calculable processes governed by immutable laws. Neither tendency is manifested in independence from its opposite, and each of the following chapters of this book will examine the impact of these interrelated tendencies on one another, and on the resulting possibilities for our understanding of animal life.

In order to examine these tendencies, manifested in concepts such as evolutionary divergence and decimation, pathology, and non-life, and to approach the problem of our often violent treatment of animals – its links as well as possibilities for thinking about alternative ways of relating to other species – this book incorporates five thematic strands, all of which are implied throughout the book, though some will come into sharper focus in different chapters.

The insights of Canguilhem, which I have touched on above, form the basis for the first theme of this book, concerning 'pathological life', and it will also serve as a means for problematising the following four strands.

VITALISM IN PHILOSOPHY AND THE LIFE SCIENCES

Chapter 1 will commence with perhaps the most generalised terms within which to consider the relation between human and animal life, deployed by Henri Bergson in his reflections on evolutionary theory. Bergson's theory of creative evolution describes the course of developments, arrests (in evolutionary bottlenecks and dead-ends), and, in more general terms, the 'tendencies' of an original impulsion, or an *élan vital*. One effect of this analysis is a displacement of the human subject from the top of traditionally conceived hierarchies of organic form and function. Bergson cites in *Creative Evolution* (1907), two interlinked aims, (a) to illuminate a theory of knowledge and a theory of life, and (b) to reveal their inseparability. These aims underpin his critique of nineteenth-century biology in a theory of human intelligence as both the product of the evolution of animal life and the distorted form of perception that is perfectly fitted for the manipulation of the material environment in accordance with function, but less so for interpreting the conditions of its own emergence. Thus Chapter 1 will be concerned with setting out the main features of evolutionary change (divergence and decimation) that dominate the theories of both Bergson and his predecessors. Chapter 2 will then focus on the limitations of human perception, and how this is manifested in the development of a certain kind of medical perception that has come to define present-day medical practice, as set out in Foucault's study of the birth of clinical medicine in the nineteenth century, with particular emphasis on the concept of *pathological life*. There, I will conclude my discussion of the second aspect of Bergson's philosophy, the development of a theory of knowledge (its possibilities and limitations in intellectual habit), by tracing the influence of the physiological studies of Xavier Bichat and Claude Bernard both on physio-pathology in general and on Bergson's theory of perception.

THE RELATION BETWEEN THE TERMS 'HUMAN' AND 'ANIMAL'

How are we to define the emerging discipline of 'animal studies'? We could, with Cary Wolfe, think this area of study in terms of the question, 'What is posthumanism?' As Wolfe observes in his 2010 work of the same name, 'posthumanism' is so diffuse a term, with often competing meanings, that the effort of defining it itself requires the exploration of many complex and intertwining histories of ideas, scientific and technological developments, and political movements. One could thus look for an understanding of posthumanism in the implications of cybernetic and information theory 'that removed the human and *Homo sapiens* from any particularly privileged position in relation to matters of meaning, information, and cognition'.[10] Alternatively, the posthumanist project could be seen as one of critique and disruption, as set out in Donna Haraway's writings on cyborgs and, later, companion species. It may also be concerned with projects of human enhancement – the 'transhumanist' expression of the possibilities open to us for achieving intellectual and physical capacities, through technological advancement, far beyond those endowed to us through the normal course of evolutionary development.[11] Animal studies, then, according to Wolfe, takes on new inflections or nuances if it is considered under the shifting lights of posthumanist thinking. It does so on two specific levels: 'not just the level of content, thematics, and the object of knowledge (the "animal" studied by animal studies) but also the level of theoretical and methodological approach (*how* animal studies studies "the animal")'.[12] Wolfe detects an immediate difficulty, for example, in the humanist tendency towards a pluralism that would ultimately result in the incorporation of its 'others' into the sphere of ethical consideration (animals are, in many ways, 'just like us'; therefore, we should grant them some level of equal treatment).

More generally, he also warns of the possible institution of intellectual habits (in this case, an anthropic perspective unaware of its own anthropocentrism) even in this field of contemporary animal studies, which is dominated by the endeavour to give a voice to creatures that have no voice:

> Just because we direct our attention to the study of nonhuman animals, and even if we do so with the aim of exposing how they have been misunderstood and exploited, that does not mean that we are not continuing to be humanist – and therefore, by definition, anthropocentric. Indeed, one of the hallmarks of humanism – and even more specifically that kind of humanism called liberalism – is its penchant for that kind of pluralism, in which the sphere of attention and consideration (intellectual or ethical) is broadened and extended to previously marginalized groups, but without in the least destabilizing or throwing into radical question the schema of the human who undertakes such pluralization.[13]

Here, Wolfe happens to summarise what I see as the problematic position of traditional moral philosophies on the question of our treatment of other animals. Essentially, moral thinking betrays a tendency to focus on the re-institution of kinds, and a questioning of the respects in which animals are sufficiently like humans to allow them into the circle of moral consideration, or which animals deserve greater consideration than others (for example, the great apes, or dogs, based on our perception of their relative intelligence).

In a follow-up work, *Before the Law* (2013), Wolfe develops his response to this humanist or liberal approach to animal studies (as ethics) in dialogue with Foucauldian biopolitics (with particular focus on the writings of Robert Esposito), addressing the relative paucity of research on animal life in terms of the exercise of biopower. Thinking animal life in biopolitical terms, Wolfe argues, cross-cuts species boundaries such that the fates of the billions of animals farmed and killed for food each year can be considered no longer simply as an ethical issue, but as one also concerning human health. In this vein, we can think of the relative harms caused by over-consumption of meat, and the introduction of new pathogens into the human population from diseased animals (for example, BSE and 'bird flu'). Or we can think about the apparent correlation between the prophylactic use of antibiotics in healthy farm animals and the increase in antibiotic-resistant strains of bacteria in humans (for example, MRSA).[14] We could also consider the impact of farming practices on the environment, and the unsustainability of such practices in the light of projected growths in the human population over the next few decades. Wolfe points to the example of synthetic meat (cultivated *in vitro*) as one possible response and solution to the manifold problems arising from intensive farming, and one that invokes a different set of ethico-political issues if considered from a biopolitical perspective:

> From this vantage, synthetic meat might not even appear to be an 'animal' issue per se, and would instead be seen as utterly continuous with the technologies and *dispositifs* that are exercising a more and more finely tuned control over life and 'making live' at the most capillary levels of social existence. Indeed, it would seem continuous with the practices of domestication, manipulation, and control of life that characterize the factory farms to which, from an animal rights point of view, it seems opposed.[15]

In Chapter 3, I will examine the contributions that thinkers in the Continental tradition (Derrida, Deleuze, Foucault) have made to this thinking of animality and the various uses to which we put non-human animals. I will consider in particular the moments of rupture or resistance that their concepts of animal life represent, and the possibilities they present for an understanding of the human-animal relation that does not simply anthropomorphise animals, but instead continues one of the trajectories I am tracing throughout this work of 'animalising' (or, more generally, de-centralising) the human subject. This will lead to a consideration of the respects in which the terms 'violence' and 'pathos' signify the status of animals in the disciplines of philosophy and the life sciences.

SCIENTIFIC IDEOLOGY

The study of scientific ideology takes into account the impact of socio-political milieus on scientific concepts, here, for example, focusing on particular examples in the life sciences and their effects on our understanding of animal life. This book covers aspects of different philosophers' methods of analysis that might be said to contribute to an 'ideological' study of the concepts of animality and organic life more broadly, but it is not exclusively a history of these ideas, nor is it simply a history of the life sciences from the nineteenth-century onwards. Comprehensive studies of the history of evolutionary theory are exemplified by Madeleine Barthélemy-Madaule, in *Lamarck the Mythical Precursor* (1982), who examines the place of Jean-Baptiste Lamarck in the history of evolutionary science from the perspective of scientific ideology, which is to say as a scientist whose ideas were embedded in the social, political and philosophical ideas of his time, as much as in the analyses he undertook within the confines of his own discipline.[16] Stephen Jay Gould's *The Structure of Evolutionary Theory* (2002) remains a staggering work in the history of science in both its depth and the consistency of its argumentation.[17] The present book is, rather more modestly, a study of certain 'tendencies', incorporating aspects of the above histories in which concepts of the animal are manifested, developed and suppressed in the works of a selected lineage of thinkers who belong to what I call a neo-vitalist trajectory spanning the nineteenth and twentieth centuries (Bergson, Whitehead, Canguilhem, Foucault, Haraway). Bergson contends that human intelligence 'is characterised by a natural inability to comprehend life',[18] and the thinkers that follow him on this trajectory all, in distinctive ways, both explore and suggest ways of overcoming this incapacity, through their own approaches to history, life and method.

In this vein, Chapter 4 will concentrate on two concepts. The first is the concept of 'non-life' that Canguilhem identifies in his ideological analysis of Darwin's theory of evolution; I will go on to argue that the 'devitalisation of life' that this represents has been carried over into the present day in the incorporation of information theory into biological explanation. The second key concept, or rather dualism, emerges here, between machine and organism. Canguilhem speculates on the possibilities of reversing the hierarchy of mechanical over organic explanation in the study of animal life, followed by Donna Haraway's turn to the image of the cyborg as a tool for the feminist critique of science and technology. The latter reveals a different sense in which the machine-organism dichotomy has been displaced: in a new understanding of the organic as coded communication system.

PROCESS PHILOSOPHY AND RETHINKING THE NATURE OF RELATION

The idea of relation that I will consider in Chapter 5 concerns the idea of 'connectedness', as stated very simply by Alfred North Whitehead in *Adventures of Ideas*: 'When we examine the universe, we discover layers of order that can either be considered in terms of their mutual interactions, or in terms of their unified impact on the experience of an external perceiver.'[19] The re-inscription of the organic, in priority over the mechanical, can be credited to both process thought and to biological complexity theory. First, Whitehead's philosophy of organism will offer a way of comprehending the basis of life not in a reductionist universal mechanism, but in a concept of organic structure that operates at all levels of reality, in a multiplicity of subjective and objective relations that are in processes of composition and decomposition prior to our habitual ascriptions of subject or object status to things or persons. Second, in Stuart Kauffman's more recent attack on mechanical reductionism, we will see an attempt to defend the specificity of biological processes, not just as an adjunct to the immutable laws of physics, but as a spur to reconfigure and expand these laws in recognition of the need for a more flexible form of scientific enquiry.

Chapter 6 features all of the above-mentioned themes, though this is not to suggest that Donna Haraway's work is in any way the culminating point or ideal synthesis of the preceding thinkers' analyses (indeed, this would be to commit the very fallacy of evolutionary thinking with which this book commences and which it criticises through the writings of Bergson). Chapter 5, on Whitehead's philosophy, is, however, positioned as a requisite for Chapter 6 on Haraway's incorporation of Derridean and Foucauldian ideas together with Whitehead's theory of prehensions as a means of defining what it means to be a 'companion animal'. This final chapter constitutes more an effort to broach, and bring to some conclusion, the question of our treatment of non-human animals in view of the movements detailed over the course of Chapters 1 to 5. For example, I will discuss how Haraway's history of the science of primatology recalls in particular instances Canguilhem's identification of a scientific tendency to create analogues of its objects in order to study them. Haraway reflects, in this vein, on the construction of animals as scientific-technical objects (for example, the 'analogue of love' in Harry Harlow's rhesus monkey experiments on mother-infant dynamics). The theory of prehensions takes on a particular significance here, in so far as it fragments human subjectivity by basing experience on the connectedness of things (as opposed to the unity of subjectivity) and recomposes relations between otherwise diverse or seemingly incompatible objects, beings or groups. In this light, I will examine the possibilities in Haraway's writings (for example, in what she calls 'nonmimetic sharing') for thinking and promoting more responsive, responsible and compassionate relationships with other animal species, even in the context of the laboratory. This will, however, prove to be far from problematic in the case of the lives of transgenic animals and, more widely, of domesticated animals, which oscillate between their status as human property, on the one hand, and their possible subjectivity, as living beings, on the other. The complex interplay of categorisations of animal life explored in this book manifests itself in the indefinable status of animal lives brought into being for the purposes of scientific research.

NOTES

1. For information on the history of this monument, see <http://www.animalsinwar.org.uk> (last accessed 8 December 2013).
2. Available at <http://www.buav.org/article/1146> (last accessed 3 December 2013).
3. Kelly Oliver, 'What Is Wrong with (Animal) Rights?', *The Journal of Speculative Philosophy*, 22:3, 2008, p. 222.
4. Ibid.
5. Kari Weil, *Thinking Animals* (New York: Columbia University Press, 2012), p. 5.
6. Georges Canguilhem, *The Normal and the Pathological* (New York: Zone Books, 1991), pp. 23–4
7. Ibid., p. 35; p. 42.
8. Ibid., p. 118.
9. Ibid., p. 182.
10. Cary Wolfe, *What is Posthumanism?* (Minneapolis: University of Minnesota Press, 2010), p. xii.
11. Ibid., p. xiii.
12. Ibid., p. 99.
13. Ibid.
14. Cary Wolfe, *Before the Law* (Chicago: University of Chicago Press, 2013) pp. 48–9.
15. Ibid., pp. 96–7.

16. Madeleine Barthélemy-Madaule, *Lamarck the Mythical Precursor* (Cambridge, MA: The MIT Press, 1982).

17. Stephen Jay Gould, *The Structure of Evolutionary Theory* (Cambridge, MA and London: The Belknap Press of Harvard University Press, 2002).

18. Henri Bergson, *Creative Evolution* (New York: Dover, 1998), p. 165.

19. Alfred North Whitehead, *Adventures of Ideas* (New York: The Free Press, [1933] 1967), p. 199.

1. *Forces of Nature: Evolution, Divergence, Decimation*

> A universe that is 'full', in the sense of exhibiting the maximal diversity of kinds, must be chiefly full of 'leaps'. There is at every point an abrupt passage to something different, and there is no purely logical principle determining – out of all the infinitely various 'possible' kinds of differentness – which shall come next.[1]

In the spirit of Alfred North Whitehead's characterisation of the history of philosophy, Arthur O. Lovejoy sets out a history of the idea of the Great Chain of Being as, essentially, a series of 'footnotes to Plato'.[2] By this he means, in particular, the predominance of thinking in terms of the principles of plenitude, of continuity, and of unilinear gradation, terms that were not fully formulated by Plato, but that nevertheless came to represent significant cornerstones of the study of natural history in subsequent eras. According to the principle of plenitude,

> the universe is a *plenum formarum* in which the range of conceivable diversity of *kinds* of living things is exhaustively exemplified, . . . that the extent and abundance of the creation must be as great as the possibility of existence and commensurate with the productive capacity of a 'perfect' and inexhaustible Source, and that the world is the better, the more things it contains.[3]

The principle of continuity, in some ways a development of the idea of plenitude, then comes to dominate natural history as the idea that all living things exist in an ascending series of forms.[4] Finally, the principle of unilinear gradation (through Aristotle), adds to the ideas of the fullness and continuity of beings the sense of their existence and organisation into hierarchies of physical and psychological development.[5]

To preface my discussion of some key debates in nineteenth-century biology, it is worth noting some aspects of eighteenth-century thought that Lovejoy identifies as having a particular effect on this idea of the Chain of Being and its basis in the Platonic principles. Lovejoy notes that, whereas the fields of astronomy, physics and metaphysics had thrown off the yoke of Aristotelianism, biology in the early modern period was characterised by a certain fidelity to Aristotle's categorisation of living things into kinds. What the eighteenth century saw, however, was the demise in the habit of thinking life in terms of species and the concomitant separation of human beings from the rest of nature.[6] Furthermore, Lovejoy continues, in line with the principle of continuity that persisted in this age, the search for *missing links* came to dominate scientific enquiry, with particular emphasis on discovering the link between plants and minerals at the lower end of the scale, and apes and humans at the higher end.[7] Finally, the invention of the microscope and the growth of the science of microbiology:

> had two conflicting effects upon men's imaginations and their feeling about the world they lived in. On the one hand, there was something highly sinister about it; it presented the ghastly spectacle of a universal parasitism, of life everywhere preying upon life, and of the human body itself as infested with myriads of tiny predatory creatures which made of it their food and sometimes – as soon began to be conjectured – their eventual victim. On the other hand, it seemed to afford additional and very striking illustrations of the prodigious fecundity of Nature and at the same time of her admirable thrift. Life, it seemed, was ubiquitous.[8]

Ultimately, Lovejoy argues that this history of the idea of the Great Chain of Being is the history of a failure.[9] It failed as an enterprise for the simple reason that our existence is temporal, and it would be the Romantic thought of philosophers such as Schelling and, later, Bergson, that would see the conversion of the Chain of Being into universal Becoming, and the displacement of the idea of *permanence* (as the ground of plenitude) by the idea of all things *in process*. Specifically, Henri Bergson's theory of vital 'tendency' argues that the diversity of life is the 'goal' of the *élan vital*, that is, the proliferation of living organisms gives expression to the ontological priority of the process of accumulation and expenditure of energy. However, also entailed in Bergson's complementary theories of life and of knowledge is the constant risk of the failure to create new lines of activity and thought. In both organic evolution and the evolution of ideas, there is a tendency to fall into habitual, that is, pathological, modes of expression. Thus, in so far as living beings tend to lose their 'immediate contact' with the real, a model of pathological functioning is integral to Bergson's thought.

In the following two chapters, two senses of 'pathological life' will come into play, one at the level of anatomy and physiology in which there is an ever-moving boundary between normal and pathological functioning as set out by George Canguilhem, where, as Lovejoy's summary of the reaction to microbiological research showed, what were once considered external threats (micro-organisms) soon came to be understood as constitutive of (and sometimes parasitic upon) macro-organic life (animal bodies). In these terms, discussions of pathological modes of being can also be found in Bergson's work in the account of conscious perception and the status of space and geometry in relation to thought. For Kant, space and time are a priori or transcendentally given, whereas for Bergson, space and time must be re-conceived as distinct determinations. That is, space is no longer a necessary condition for sense experience, and we must abandon our tendency to think time in spatial terms – a distinctly human pathology of thought – in order to make thought adequate to reality as process. Other animals, for example, as Bergson speculates in *Time and Free Will* (1889), might be said to perceive the world according to various non-spatial or non-geometrical 'markers' (e.g. sound, smell, or even magnetic currents):

> Naturalists have pointed out, as a remarkable fact, the surprising ease with which many vertebrates, and even some insects, manage to find their way through space. Animals have been seen to return almost in a straight line to their old home, pursuing a path which was hitherto unknown to them over a distance which may amount to several hundreds of miles. Attempts have been made to explain this feeling of direction by sight or smell, and, more recently, by the perception of magnetic currents which would enable the animal to take its bearings like a living compass. This amounts to saying that space is not so homogeneous for the animal as for us, and that determinations of space, or directions, do not assume for it a purely geometrical form. Each of these directions might appear to it with its own shade, its peculiar quality.[10]

Thus, against Kant, Bergson emphasises the separation between sensible intuitions and the form of space. The remarks on perception of extensity, which Bergson associates with instinct-dominated organisms, emphasise the possibilities, even for human consciousness (which is, after all, characterised by both instinct and intelligence), for grasping reality in non-geometrical and non-spatial terms. In Chapter 2, I will turn to a fuller analysis of the concept of 'pathological life' as developed in the medical sciences in the nineteenth century, the associated emergence of a specific kind of medical perception, and Bergson's response to some of these developments in his reconsideration of perception itself and its spatialising character as potential barrier to a proper understanding of living processes.

For the moment I want to focus on a second sense of pathological life that emerges at the level of the evolution of organic life as a whole. In it the foundations are set for thinking the boundary between normal and pathological states in the determination of advantageous or disadvantageous features. Contrary to conceptions of the Great Chain of Being in which living things are organised and coexist in an ascending series of increased perfection, the account of evolutionary development that Bergson propounds will describe an alternative *telos* of life that incorporates greater amounts of diversity and unbounded creativity than either mechanical causality or 'anthropomorphic finality' allow. This evolution of living organisms as a history that is definable in terms of its failures as much as the triumph of the fittest organisms will be the main focus of the present chapter. Or rather, we can consider the implications of thinking life no longer as the movement towards greater perfection, but as a much more contingent explosion of diverse complex forms. Today, what we think of as the diversity of life applies at the level of *species* (under a relatively sparse range of phyla), and Stephen Jay Gould will subsequently argue, for example, that the fossil record indicates that diversity at the level of *phyla* has existed much earlier in the history of organic life than the traditional models of evolutionary progress would suggest, thereby challenging the model of evolutionary development which commences with a small number of common ancestors.

I will begin, in the following discussion of Bergson's *Creative Evolution*, with two aspects of Bergson's evolutionism, and his idiosyncratic taxonomical description of the plant and animal kingdoms, that have their basis in some famous debates in the biological sciences of the nineteenth century: firstly, the debate between Georges Cuvier and Étienne Geoffroy Saint-Hilaire on the divisions of the animal kingdom in line with either function or form, which is often cited as an early manifestation of evolutionary thinking prior to Darwin, but which will be taken here primarily as a debate about the limits of taxonomical description;[11] secondly, the debate between August Weismann and Theodor Eimer on the nature and modes of transmission of characteristics (transmutation), after Darwin. Bergson's philosophy meditates on the limitations of human thought, for example in the persistence of certain interpretations of the empirical data, such as the tree or cone models of evolution as progress towards increasing complexity and towards its 'ideal' in the human form, an ideal that is a retroactively imposed anthropomorphism of the process of evolutionary development.

TAXONOMY AND DIRECTED DEVELOPMENT

In his *Animal Kingdom* (1817), Cuvier proceeds to divide and re-categorise animal life according to a set of anatomical characteristics that fall into four basic body plans, or *embranchements*: Vertebrata, Mollusca, Articulata and Radiata.[12] Of central importance in this description of the specific nature of the kingdom Animalia is first a founding distinction between plants and animals in terms of *capacity for movement*.[13] Animals have developed a range of physiological processes and anatomical characters that compensate for lacking the ability to manufacture food from sources in their immediate surroundings, as plants are able to do. In addition, the four key characters of animal bodies (animation, circulation, complex chemical composition, and respiration) all demonstrate the basis of animal life in the varying development of a sensory-motor system which allows it to access and utilise energy in its surrounding environment.[14] Finally, Cuvier notes that the characteristics mentioned above give rise to varying levels of intellectual and instinctive functions in animals:

> Although, with respect to the intellectual faculties, the most perfect animals are infinitely beneath man; it is certain that their intelligence performs operations of the same kind. They move in consequence of sensations received, are susceptible of durable affections, and acquire by experience a certain knowledge of things, by which they are governed independently of actual pain or pleasure, and by the simple foresight of consequences.[15]

Instincts, on the other hand, are firmly characteristic of species (e.g. bees and wasps) and seem to indicate the existence of 'innate and perpetual images or sensations'[16] that compel actions to be performed in the same way, and which point to the operation of life 'as a kind of somnambulism'.[17] Cuvier's descriptions ground both the unity of design (the four body plans) and diversity of adaptations on a functionalist interpretation: that is, in accordance with the requirements of the sensory-motor or nervous system.[18]

Turning to Geoffroy, the formalist argument put forward in his 1818 work, *Philosophie Anatomique*, resolved animal phyla into a unity of type based on the vertebrate skeleton.[19] Geoffroy's key arguments against Cuvier are also summarised in his *Principes de Philosophie Zoologique* (1830). Using observations on the skeletons of fishes, which are sufficiently divergent from those of other animals to present a special obstacle to the theory of unity of type, Geoffroy makes significant advances in the identification of anatomical homologies.[20] Thus what appear to be radical divergences of form between most vertebrate animals and fishes can be explained and rendered uniform by noting the similarities in spatial organisation and relative positioning of organs and limbs: 'Parts may expand and contract according to utility, but topology remains unaltered, and the archetype can be traced by unvarying spatial order.'[21]

At first glance, Geoffroy's formalist approach to animal anatomy would seem to align well with the Bergsonian derogation of utility-driven thought and its tendency to project its bias towards function back onto nature. Just because human thought tends to carve up reality in order to better exercise its influence upon it, this does not allow us to ascribe such distinctions to things in the world, to time itself, in their actuality. Reality (Life and Matter) begins as one, and thought divides it. However, it is to Cuvier's division of animal life according to function that Bergson appeals in his idiosyncratic taxonomy presented in the second chapter of *Creative Evolution*. Where Bergson diverges most significantly from Cuvier's work is in his emphasis on the special role of habit as a form of activity, acquired and expressed at the level of individual organisms. Cuvier specifically rejects habits or other such 'momentary' properties as a means of categorising the characters (dominating or subordinate) of organisms, but we will see that this is essential to Bergson's taxonomy as a fundamental expression of the 'common impulsion' of life.

In the traditional taxonomical division of organic life, we begin with the highest level of generality (Kingdoms) and end with the most specific division (Species). For example, the main Kingdoms are: Plantae, Animalia, Fungi, Protista, Monera. The main phyla include Animalia, under which we find arthropods (insects and crustaceans) and chordates (vertebrates). Starting with the model of organic evolution that he presents in his 1907 work, *Creative Evolution*, Bergson's aim is to rethink the mechanism of evolution according to a kind of classification of 'activity'. The most general kind of activity occurs by virtue of 'the resistance life meets from inert matter, and the explosive force – due to an unstable balance of tendencies – which life bears within itself'.[22] The accumulation and expenditure of energy then gives rise to a division of labour between (roughly) plants and animals: plants accumulate potential energy through photosynthesis. Their ability to manufacture their own food allows this organic line to 'dispense with movement and so with feeling'.[23] All other creatures release that energy 'explosively' through movement, their need to search for food giving rise to variations in locomotor activity and greater intensities of consciousness.[24] Following this is a continual process of division of tendency along divergent lines, one example being what Bergson tentatively calls an impulse towards social life, which is the most visible in the hymenoptera (ants, bees, etc.) on the one hand, and human beings on the other.[25] Finally, at the level of animal life (in arthropods and chordates), a division between instinct and intelligence emerges.[26]

In this set of divisions, Bergson is answering what he calls the 'cardinal error' (from Aristotle onwards) of interpreting vegetative, instinctive and rational life as three successive phases of the development of life (what we might call a tendency towards rationality, or human consciousness). For Bergson, these divisions really constitute 'divergent directions of an activity that has split up as it grew. The difference between them is not a difference of intensity, nor, more generally, of degree, but of kind.'[27] Furthermore, in order to argue against the account of evolution as the progressive accumulation of characteristics, achieved through association and convergence of effort (Lamarckian and some Darwinian accounts), Bergson prioritises dissociation and 'divergence of efforts'.[28] 'Tendency', in Bergson's sense, puts forward both a model of evolution in accordance with a common impulsion (*élan vital*), but one that manifests itself along divergent lines. Evolution is *not* progress towards fewer and better, offering us the temptation to think of human beings as somehow the most perfected of complex organisms. Rather, the common impulsion, what we might call the impulse of material life (life meeting matter, though this distinction between the two is simply for the purposes of expression) has happened to give rise to *Homo sapiens*, but it is, as Bergson goes on to explain, a process that is continual, and is likely to continue beyond human life.[29]

Despite Cuvier's 'victory' over Geoffroy (and his animosity towards Lamarck), Bergson seeks to defend an ontological monism underpinning any material divisions that might exist. This might remain compatible with Cuvier's functionalism, if we consider the material and empirical facts of animal divisions (of labour) underpinned by a unity of *process* (process supplants being, as ontological basis). The debate between August Weismann and Theodor Eimer gives us an expression of this unity in the development of evolutionary theory after Darwin.

At the heart of the debate between Eimer and Weismann is a disagreement about the nature of possibility and the reliance of any theory of natural *selection* upon it: Weismann argues that the different possible avenues of evolution open to an organism (at the level of individual characteristics that are guided by function) are carried in the germ-plasm. For Eimer, this is an absurdity which ignores the key role of environmental influence in adaptation. Weismann defends his theory of the germ-plasm against critics of it, including Eimer, for its inadequacy as a theory of evolution, that is, as a theory of development.[30] Against this criticism, Weismann reiterates that the germ-plasm is postulated to account only for *heredity*, or the vehicle for the transmission of characteristics. In the absence of actual evidence of this vehicle of heredity (with DNA to remain undiscovered until the next century) Weismann appeals to the 'the scientific import of imagination'[31] in other disciplines, such as physics and chemistry, and puts forward two 'representative models' designed to aid, through analogical description, our understanding of the possible mechanisms at work in heredity:

> the *determinants*, which may be conceived as indefinitely fashioned packages of units (biophores) which are set into activity by definite impressions and put a distinctive stamp upon some small part of the organism, on some cell or group of cells, evoking definite phenomena somewhat as a piece of fireworks when lighted produces a brilliant sun, a shower of sparks, or the glowing characters of a name.
>
> The *ids*, also, are such representative models, and may be compared to a definitely ordered but variously compounded aggregate of fireworks, in which the single pieces are so connected as to go off in fixed succession and to produce a definite resultant phenomenon like a complete inscription surrounded by a hail of fire and glowing spheres.[32]

In order to illustrate next the *efficacy* of natural selection (in Darwinian terms) Weismann assumes that a large number of possible variations come into being, and it is *utility* that determines which variations will be selected. It is these two key aspects of natural selection that Eimer will attempt to refute, and the argument between the two biologists centres on explanations of how and why the markings on the wings of different species of butterfly vary, and the extent to which their environmental conditions affect these variations. For Weismann, who is replying explicitly to Eimer, and other proponents of 'teleological explanation', examples of butterflies whose wings have come to resemble the leaves of trees indigenous to the forests they inhabit (e.g. Kallima Inachis, and Parallecta, the 'Indian leaf butterflies') clearly show that such a large range of variations 'must have always been present' in order to result in the selection of markings that coincide with the leaf patterns.[33] Other examples that Weismann cites are the apparatuses in divergent varieties of plants used for capturing small animals, and, more commonly, the many versions, at widely differing levels of complexity, of eyes across different species. All of these adaptations have in common the 'profound connection' between the utility of the variation and its emergence in different forms, which, for Weismann, indicates the determination of variations by utility.[34]

The influence of utility is central to Eimer's objections to Weismann, and he sets out to refute what he sees as the three main contentions of the theory of the germ-plasm. The first contention of germ-plasm theory concerns the nature of possibility: characters are selected from a pool of 'all possible characters'. Eimer responds that useful characters do not always arise, thus selection cannot be the primary driver of evolution. Referring back to the example of the Indian leaf butterflies, Eimer cites the experiments (of Standfuss) in which heat is applied to developing pupae of northern European species, and these result in variations in the fully developed insects that are equivalent to butterflies found in southern climates. The action of heat and light in this way can also then give rise to an inheritance of the *acquired* characteristics in future generations (against Weismann's explanations for colour variation).[35] What Eimer finds lacking in Weismann is an acknowledgement of the sudden appearance 'in approximate perfection' of a useful adaptation. It is the whole organism (not just any one part) considered in its environment (function, activity, and a definitely directed evolution) that must be taken into account in an explanation of evolutionary development.[36]

Eimer's second argument against Weismann is that it is not the case *that the directions of evolutionary development are selected*; they too have nothing to do with utility. Definitely directed evolution, or the sudden appearance of complex adaptive features, is not, for Eimer, determined by utility. This is evidenced, for example, by the appearance of many 'useless' characteristics in animals that provide them with no clear advantage in their habitats. Rather, their morphological changes simply tend to reflect their 'varying outward conditions of life'.[37] Weismann's third key contention is that once the many variations arise, selection takes place around a 'zero-point'; any particular change can diverge so far until either a new species can be said to have been formed, or until the change becomes deleterious to the survival or general effective functioning of the organism.[38] Against this, Eimer propounds his theory of directed development that advances in a straight line, with some divergences. On such a view, the origin of species can be explained in terms of a limited number of causes, including: 'genepistasis', or the cessation of development at particular stages of evolution; and 'halmatogenesis', the 'sudden, unsolicited appearance of new characters, or, where a large number of such new characters appear, of the sudden origin of new forms that deviate widely from the ancestral form'.[39]

BERGSON'S EVOLUTIONISM

In the first chapter of *Creative Evolution*, Bergson's responses to Weismann and Eimer are more generous to both biologists than they are to one another, and the relative merits of each theory are, as Bergson points out, weighed up in the spirit of a form of philosophical enquiry that does not require the exactitude of the sciences, but that can incorporate many 'partial views' of a particular problem.[40] Bergson's responses to these, and other, theorists incorporate the problems of continuity (both within the organism and between individuals), the directionality of evolution, and the role of environmental influence into what he sees as a unifying theory of a common impulsion or the *élan vital*. More than simply a return to pre-nineteenth-century vitalist and animist theories, the vital impetus is presented as the metaphysical complement to the biological theories discussed, and one that exposes their common ground.

Bergson distinguishes himself from the tradition of finalism or teleology (which includes Leibniz and Kant) through his own special sense of neo-vitalism as an 'external finality'. Where traditional finalist thinking tended towards the ultimately problematic ascription of purposiveness to individual organisms, describing an 'internal finality' in which 'each being is made for itself, all its parts conspire for the greatest good of the whole and are intelligently organised in view of that end',[41] an *external* finality exerts an influence on the organisation of individual organisms in relation to one another. Factors other than a force or drive internal to each organism would need to be considered in order to provide a theory that encompasses both the trajectories of species along divergent lines of evolution and their convergence in particular instances. The existence of an external finality would, for example, explain the phenomenon of convergent evolution, where organs with similar functions evolve in radically distinct species (compare the eyes of mammals with the compound eyes of insects).[42]

In Weismann's work, as we saw above, the theory of the germ-plasm is a description of the vehicle of heredity, but does not explain (nor does it attempt to) the origin or emergence of variations, let alone the convergence of function along different evolutionary paths. For Bergson, the usefulness of Weismann's theory is in the identification of variability at the level of the germinal cells independently of the activities and experiences of the individual. What is problematic for Bergson (as for Eimer) is the idea that such variations are either insensible or sudden and accidental, giving rise to the pool of possible characteristics from which actual lines of evolution are selected. He turns to a consideration of the limitations of Weismann's theory in contrast to theories of the transmission of acquired characteristics, though he will show that the introduction of some idea of 'effort' cannot take the form of the individual effort of organisms favoured by Lamarck, but rather in a combination of Eimer's thought and Bergson's own version of finalism. To illustrate, Bergson first appeals to certain experiments that have appeared to demonstrate the transmission of acquired characteristics: here, the experiments of the nineteenth-century physician and physiologist Charles-Édouard Brown-Séquard, demonstrating a condition of sensory loss resulting from spinal injury that now bears his name,[43] but at the time was claimed by Brown-Séquard to also result in the inheritance of the same condition in the offspring of the injured individual:

> By cutting the spinal cord or the sciatic nerve of guinea-pigs, Brown-Séquard brought about an epileptic state which was transmitted to the descendants. Lesions of the same sciatic nerve, of the restiform body, etc., provoked various troubles in the guinea-pig which its progeny inherited sometimes in a quite different form: exophthalmia, loss of toes, etc. But it is not demonstrated that in these different cases of hereditary transmission there had been a real influence of the soma of the animal on its germ-plasm. Weismann at once objected that the operations of Brown-Séquard might have introduced certain special microbes into the body of the guinea-pig, which had found their means of nutrition in the nervous tissues and transmitted the malady by penetrating into the sexual elements.[44]

Bergson rejects Brown-Séquard's claim that the morbid condition itself has been inherited by the offspring of the injured guinea pigs. Rather, he puts forward as more likely the hypothesis of a natural disposition that existed in the individual prior to the apparent transmission of certain characteristics that can essentially be described as 'habits', or previously conscious actions repeated over time that come to be performed unconsciously. This natural disposition, Bergson argues, would explain the apparent transmission of acquired characteristics, since the disposition towards certain behaviour was already in the individual and would require less specific conditions than the acquisition of particular behaviours in order to manifest itself in later generations. It would also remain compatible with Weismann's theory of the germ-plasm (or any theory of the vehicle of heredity) as this pre-existing disposition is transmitted from the generation of the injured individual (or individual with the acquired characteristic) to subsequent generations: 'Thus, for instance, there is no proof that the mole has become blind because it has formed the habit of living underground; it is perhaps because its eyes were becoming atrophied that it condemned itself to a life underground.'[45] Bergson's alternative is, then, a more generalised explanation for heredity than the transmission of acquired characters, but a more 'directed' or teleological theory than Weismann's germ-plasm. As Bergson explains:

> It might therefore be said that, though the germ-plasm is not continuous, there is at least continuity of genetic energy, this energy being expended only at certain instants, for just enough time to give the requisite impulsion to the embryonic life, and being recouped as soon as possible in new sexual elements, in which, again, it bides its time. Regarded from this point of view, *life is like a current passing from germ to germ through the medium of a developed organism*. It is as if the organism itself were only an excrescence,

a bud caused to sprout by the former germ endeavouring to continue itself in a new germ.[46]

The final component of Bergson's theory of the *élan vital*, in which the influence of Eimer's work can be felt, is that of environmental effects on adaptation. Bergson notes that differing senses of adaptation are employed by biologists, but that these tend to fall under two main categories: the *direct* and *indirect* responses to changes in environmental conditions.[47] Direct adaptation is essentially mechanical adjustment of a material to fit into its environment, for example in the cases of two liquids, say, water and wine, poured into the same glass. Both liquids will adopt the same form in order to fit into the same container. Indirect adaptation is, on the other hand, a *creative* form of adaptation in which the living being's solution to the problem of the new environmental conditions does not simply entail a mechanical adjustment of itself to those conditions:

> It will have to make the best of these circumstances, neutralise their inconveniences and utilise their advantages – in short, respond to outer actions by building up a machine which has no resemblance to them. Such adapting is not repeating, but replying, – an entirely different thing. If there is still adaptation, it will be in the sense in which one may say of the solution of a problem of geometry, for example, that it is adapted to the conditions.[48]

The levels and complexity of responsiveness of an organism to its environment required to evolve new, advantageous characteristics are, for Bergson, comparable to the creative responsiveness of a consciousness in the activity of problem-solving. Two essays by Bergson, published in his collection *Mind-Energy* (1919), helpfully summarise the affinities between life and consciousness and indeed the necessity to think both processes as expressions of the same movement, the *élan vital*.

First of all, in 'Intellectual Effort', Bergson provides a model that will help us to distinguish between mechanical and creative adaptation in terms of *different levels of consciousness*, and commences his explanation by distinguishing two modes of recollection. The first involves the mechanical retention of visual or auditory images, and their recollection. We tend to employ both 'mechanical' and 'intellectual' forms of memory in order to recall something we have learnt, and thus cannot normally say where one starts and the other ends in such attempts. However, Bergson characteristically points to some instances in which the two types of 'retention' and recall are made distinct. Examples of 'memory habits' include that based on vision such as the learning or retention, through repetition, of many elements within a single glance, enabling one to recount a large number of those elements at a later point (e.g. the titles and order of books in a bookcase, or objects in a shop window, etc.).[49] In this kind of memory education, 'All interpretation of the visual image was excluded from the act of seeing. The mind was kept on the plane of visual images.'[50] An auditory example might be that of learning a new language 'mechanically', repeating whole sentences aloud without also knowing what they mean. Gradually, the meaning will be discerned through learning different combinations of words until the meaning surfaces through repetition rather than the direct concentration of understanding.

As Bergson postulated in *Matter and Memory*, there are multiple planes of consciousness, and all of the above kinds of recall (visual, auditory, as well as motor) take place on the *plane of sensation, movement and action*: 'The object is to obtain from memory an instantaneous and easy recall, and the contrivance consists in making the mind move as much as possible among images of sounds or articulations without the more abstract elements, external to the plane of sensations and movements, intervening.'[51] When, on the other hand, some kind of effort of mind is involved in recollection, there is a movement between different planes of consciousness. In this method:

> We jump to a point where the multiplicity of the images seems to be condensed into a single, simple and undivided idea. It is this idea we commit to memory. Then, when the moment of recall comes, we redescend from the top of the pyramid towards the base. We pass from the higher plane, in which all was gathered up into a single idea, to lower and lower planes, nearer and nearer to sensation, where the simple idea is dispersed in images, and where the images develop into sentences and words.[52]

Thus we have moved from the association of images (on the plane of sensation) to a form of recollection involving different levels of memory, or in other words involving an *effort*. What allows there to be a difference between the two types of recall is, Bergson explains, the 'dynamic scheme' or an idea that does not contain the images themselves but rather suggests or indicates what we need to do to reconstruct those images. Bergson uses the example of games scenarios retained by chess-players. Here, it would not be a case of successively remembering and associating all of the individual pieces and then reconstructing them piece by piece and move by move until a whole game is reconstructed. Rather, from accounts provided by players themselves, the following stages are suggested: the pieces imply the abstract ideas of 'forces'; the idea of 'the game' becomes instead that of the interactions of these forces, and the abstract idea of each game is *one*, allowing the player to keep several games in mind at once.[53]

The two types of recall, then, involve distinct types and degrees of effort: first, sense-based recall moves 'horizontally' amongst homogeneous images (e.g. many sensory images) in order to recall many different objects; second, intellectual recall or effort moves 'vertically' amongst heterogeneous intellectual states (a mixture of sense-images and abstract schemes/ideas) in order to recall *one* object. The two types of recall are, of course, more frequently called upon at the same time, but they can be distinguished from one another in certain instances, particularly in pathological conditions. In the case of intellection without effort (or intellectual habits), Bergson cites the example of dementia to show how a sufferer of the condition can carry on a seemingly normal conversation without actually understanding their own words and meanings: words are simply strung together through the association of familiar sounds. This, for Bergson, illustrates the way in which apparently intellectual activity can remain on a single plane of consciousness.[54]

In the case of its inverse, intellectual effort, Bergson is challenging an empirical account of learning and recollection. Here, we start with the idea that taking in and interpreting new information (reading a book, hearing a talk or a piece of music) involves a movement from the uptake of sensory data to their consolidation into an intellectual or ideal form (from concrete to abstract; or from perception to memory). In any perception, on Bergson's reading, some memory is always already implicated in order for a field of images to become focused upon the relevant properties of one object for our attention and use. Thus we find, in the effort of interpretation (of a book, a talk, some music) the opposite movement, from abstract to concrete. To summarise, this voluntary form of intellection or *attention* involves a feeling of effort, or the appeal to different kinds of memory, both sensory and ideal, in order to recall an object. There is here some sort of prefiguration beyond the merely sensible image described in mechanical recall or attention. As Bergson speculates, the deployment of different levels of memory works to intensify or clarify the object or image in mind. We try to match a set of recollections to our object, and repeat the operation until the virtual image becomes adequate to the real object or action:

> The intellectual effort to interpret, to comprehend, to pay attention, is then a movement of the 'dynamic scheme' in the direction of the image which develops it. It is a continuous transformation of abstract relations, suggested by the objects perceived, into concrete images capable of recovering these objects.[55]

Building on such models of memory as the basis of conscious activity, in 'Life and Consciousness' Bergson goes on to suggest a number of 'lines of fact' that help us to draw certain conclusions about the nature of consciousness and its place in the evolution of organic life. These lines of fact include, firstly, a reiteration of the different levels of willed activity that can all be summed up as different levels of memory, as discussed in *Matter and Memory* and in the essay 'Intellectual Effort' summarised above. If memory, or the ability to conserve the past, is the basic definition of consciousness, then consciousness clearly manifests itself across a whole range of living organisms:

> If then, at the top of the scale of living beings, consciousness is attached to very complicated nervous centres, must we not suppose that it accompanies the nervous system down its whole descent, and that when at last the nerve stuff is merged in the yet undifferentiated living matter, consciousness is still there, diffused, confused, but not reduced to nothing? Theoretically, then, everything living might be conscious. *In principle*, consciousness is coextensive with life.[56]

This suggests a second line of fact relating to the degrees of consciousness, 'from attention down to slumber', that are found in different organisms in which the nervous system is constructed in diverse ways and at different levels of complexity, but all with the same purpose: to facilitate chosen actions. This is shown in the different paths that evolution has taken: in plants, lower animals, and higher animals. The further down the animal scale we descend, the less differentiated become the functions of the spinal cord and the brain.[57] At the lowest point, in the amoeba, its reactions appear to be mechanical though, even there, hesitation can be seen:

> The amoeba, for instance, when in the presence of a substance which can be made food, pushes out towards it filaments able to seize and enfold foreign bodies. These pseudopodia are real organs and therefore mechanisms; but they are only temporary organs created for the particular purpose, and it seems they still show the rudiments of choice.[58]

Thus, argues Bergson, consciousness seems to be everywhere *in right*, but sometimes renounced *in fact* (for example, in parasitic animals and most plants). In our own activities this process of consciousness becoming dormant is evident, such as in spontaneous actions that become automatic (habit). On the other hand, consciousness becomes its liveliest 'at moments of inward crisis when we hesitate between two, or it may be several, different courses to take, when we feel that our future will be what we make it'.[59] In the evolution of organic life, we can, similarly, see different stages of conscious life: Life can either take the path towards movement and action (towards freedom), which is the path towards animal life, or it can obtain from its current spot all that it requires to live (a tranquil, un-enterprising existence), the path of plant life. Furthermore, the two paths, plant and animal, though distinct in many ways, still retain traces of their alternative (arrested animal life, and mobile plant life).[60]

Finally, the third line of fact suggests that conscious activity aims towards the greatest intensity of freedom or creativity. Here, we are presented with an expression of the complementary or double aspect of the movement of life:

> In one, by an explosive action, it liberates instantly, in the chosen direction, energy which matter has been accumulating during a long time; in the other, by a work of contraction, it gathers into a single instant the incalculable number of small events which matter holds distinct, as when we sum up in a word the immensity of a history.[61]

In other words, this is an expression of life's double movement of extension and contraction, manifesting at different levels of organic life. First of all, the movements of accumulation and discharge of energy are enacted by individuals with 'higher' forms of consciousness in willed and creative acts, but then secondly, at the level of 'life in general', the movement of accumulation occurs in plant life in photosynthetic activity, while the movement of discharge of energy occurs in animal life sustained by the consumption of plants at the lowest end of the food chain. It is this broader movement to which Bergson refers when he sees 'in the whole evolution of life on our planet a crossing of matter by a creative consciousness, and effort to set free, by force of ingenuity and invention, something which in the animal still remains imprisoned and is only finally released when we reach man'.[62]

For Bergson, evolutionary theory in the nineteenth and early twentieth centuries, though compelling, seems only to bear out conclusions about the arrest of life at various points, whereas we do not see in such theories an explanation of the movement that carries organisation onwards to higher forms. Bergson responds with the suggestion of an 'impulse driving it to take ever greater and greater risks towards its goal of an ever higher and higher efficiency'.[63] Life has not proceeded in one direction, but rather split along divergent lines, with two lines, in particular, proving to be the most successful: arthropods (up to bees and ants) and vertebrates (up to human beings), but the manifestations of different levels of consciousness suggest that 'the evolving force bore within it originally, but confused together or rather the one implied in the other, instinct and intelligence'.[64] It is not, then, that the progress of evolution has been one directed towards the perfection of forms, culminating in human life (where evolution in line with internal finality compares 'the work of nature to that of an intelligent workman'[65]), nor does it manifest the plenitude of possible existing forms suggested by the idea of the Great Chain of Being. If there is continuity between living things, it is the continuity of a common impulsion of life that ensures the continual emergence of new organic forms, and this in turn manifests a continual 'renegotiation' of hierarchies within nature as different species both emerge and die out. Evolution is open, chaotic, and it is as prone to the creation of dead-ends and failures as it is to the creation of new and successful organisms.

DIVERSITY AND DECIMATION

An unexpected continuity in this line of thinking can be found in the work of the evolutionary biologist Stephen Jay Gould, who reinforces, in his writings on the fossils of the Burgess Shale, the persistence of thinking in terms of the Great Chain of Being in twentieth-century theories of evolution. The interpretations of the evolutionary implications of the Burgess fossils at the time of their discovery, Gould argues, ought to make us question the nature of taxonomical division and the influence of ideology (as intellectual and cultural bias) on scientific interpretation.

In *Wonderful Life* (1990) Gould argues for a greater appreciation of the contingency of evolutionary processes, pointing to the patterns of emergence, decimation and diversity that seem to be evidenced by the fossil find at the Burgess Shale in British Columbia. This record dates from around 530 million years ago, and represents a period just after the Cambrian explosion (very roughly, from around 570 million years ago). It indicates that a relatively large diversity of phyla ('ground plans' or 'body plans') evolves or 'explodes', followed by a period of 'decimation' of these phyla, which then gives us the limitation of phyla to four out of the twenty or so types that we recognise today. That is, out of the fifteen to twenty organisms found in Burgess (each of which, Gould argues, can be classified as distinct phyla), only three can be linked to phyla that still exist today, and one other (Trilobita) is found in later fossil records but is extinct today.[66]

Gould's book argues against both the tree and cone models of evolutionary 'progress', which have always suggested that existence later in the evolutionary process implies more complex, 'superior' and 'fitter' in a supposed genetic hierarchy. On such a model, *Homo sapiens* tends to be portrayed as a natural superior to all other organisms, which are all, technically, also the latest products of evolutionary lines.[67] Gould explains that the Burgess organisms (all arthropods, or animals of the insect and crustacean type) were 'shoehorned' into modern phyla as a consequence of the scientific and cultural prejudices of the palaeontologist who discovered the Burgess Shale, Charles Doolittle Walcott. Against this view, Gould carefully works through the anatomical characteristics of several of the most common organisms found on the

Burgess site, and argues that their distinctiveness is of such a degree that they merit classification within their own phyla, rather than within known groups (which was Walcott's shoehorning error). What this means is that such fossil records from the Cambrian period do not simply give us evolutionary ancestors for current species (although some of these do exist at Burgess), but present us with a larger than expected degree of anatomical diversity at certain points in evolutionary history. This diversity is then subjected to a period of decimation, survived only by relatively few phyla, which go on to spring their own set of divergent species though now limited to this smaller group of phyla: the resultant model, starting from the end of the decimation period, is the familiar cone of diversity which commences with a common ancestor at its narrowest point, giving rise to several 'variations on a theme' (variations of a particular phylum or anatomical 'ground plan').

Finally, Gould's argument in response to this new model of explosion, decimation and diversity of limited anatomical form, is that palaeontologists have not yet come up with good reasons as to why only certain forms survived decimation, and others did not. The key implication here is that the process of decimation appears to have been so capricious that we can best conclude that 'natural selection' is a far more contingent selector than Darwin's phrase at first implies (given its analogue in the human activity of artificial selection). The fossil record can never, of course, furnish us with enough detail to make accurate judgements about the conditions that led to the decline of an entire phylum, but Gould's argument is that the range of animal phyla existing today is not, in itself, sufficient evidence of superiority or 'fitness'. Just because *Homo sapiens* has survived, and *Homo neanderthalensis* has not, is not evidence of the superiority of the former.[68] The mistake here would be to confuse the 'entity' that has happened to survive (that is, *Homo sapiens*), with a supposed 'tendency' that we might call 'consciousness capable of representational thought'. We end up defining the former in terms of the qualities of the latter.[69] Gould argues that such retroactive judgements (exemplified by Walcott's shoehorning) obscured what was really a huge amount of contingency in the process of evolutionary selection.

What we can conclude from this, as Gould continues, is that if the evolutionary 'tape' was to rewind and replay, it is just as likely that a completely different set of phyla would have survived, and would have thus given rise to a very different set of species living today. It is quite possible that human beings might not have evolved at all. Simon Conway Morris, whose work on the Burgess organisms Gould discusses in *Wonderful Life*, subsequently argues against Gould's contingency claim, in favour of a view that the emergence of human intelligence was, to a degree, inevitable.[70] Conway Morris returns us to the phenomenon of convergent evolution which describes the emergence of like characteristics in otherwise divergent groups, such as the many different types of eyes in divergent animal groups, or the evolution of the streamlined body with fins in both fishes and cetaceans (whales and dolphins). Such convergences arise through a combination of limited genetic bases mutating against the backdrop of limited or common environmental conditions (for example, an ocean).

For Gould, then, the cone of increasing complexity can only be applied to parts of the overall development of living organisms. Key implications are (a) that complexity occurs quickly and earlier in the evolution of life on earth than traditional concepts of evolutionary progress suggest; (b) that there is no good evidence in the fossil record to explain why some phyla became extinct and those living today survived; and (c) the surviving organisms' lines of development become, then, relatively limited (at an anatomical level), which points not to increasing complexity (life's insurance against radical environmental upheaval) but rather to increasing specialisation which makes these later organisms highly dependent upon stable environmental conditions, and thus subject to a greater degree of contingency than theories of directed or purposeful evolution suggest.

In Bergsonian terms, even though the idea of 'tendency' would seem to point to some degree of necessity, his focus on the development of the human intellect is not equivalent to Conway Morris' belief in the inevitability of human life. Bergson's perspective on evolutionary theory is that it tends to reflect specialisation and limitation, but neither the human intellectual tendency to think evolution as progress to higher forms nor the inscription of particular patterns of functioning (at a genetic level) form completely closed systems. For Bergson, at the level of human consciousness the possibility remains for conceptualisation outside the strict boundaries of spatial thought, while life in general carries with it the capacity for the continual development of new and complex forms of life in its broadest movements of accumulation and expenditure of energy. Bergson's analysis of the divergent lines of evolution, exemplified by instinct and intelligence at the level of phyla (arthropods versus chordates), rids our account of evolutionary history of its anthropocentrism and its hierarchical categorisations. There is no claim in Bergson that human consciousness would always have evolved (as Conway Morris argues). Rather, we find the softer claim that life manifests itself in all kingdoms as a *negotiation* between matter and life, with the most general aim of accumulating potential energy followed by its explosive release in movement. As we saw, in both Bergson and Gould, the arrival of *Homo sapiens* is a contingent event, one that is destined to be superseded by some other form of life.

What is underlined here is the precariousness of human life, along with all other forms of life, within a wider movement of evolution that is ultimately indifferent to the successes and failures of any one of the species that it manifests along the way. In these terms, the whole of animal life – human or otherwise – is collectively characterised in terms of a common vulnerability to the interactions of internal (genetic) and environmental conditions. In the next chapter, we will see how the nineteenth century also witnessed a shift in the understanding of organic life towards an idea of inherent pathology, specifically within the context of the developing sciences of physiology and medicine, but also in line with changing attitudes towards the nature and limits of perception itself. The living organism must no longer simply be understood as subject to inherited propensities or environmental changes, but rather as susceptible to, and defined by, its own progress towards disease and death.

NOTES

1. Arthur O. Lovejoy, *The Great Chain of Being* (Cambridge, MA: Harvard University Press, 1964), p. 332.
2. Ibid., p. 326.
3. Ibid., p. 52.
4. Ibid., p. 56.
5. Ibid., p. 59.
6. Ibid., p. 231.
7. Ibid., pp. 234–5. Some of this enquiry, Lovejoy notes, led to scrutiny of 'remote peoples' who could be categorised as only semi-human, whilst Rousseau, amongst others, preferred to assert that humans and apes in fact belonged to the same species, and that language was simply an acquired facility learnt by one group within that species.
8. Ibid., p. 238.
9. Ibid., p. 329.
10. Bergson, *Time and Free Will* (New York: Dover, 2001), p. 96.
11. Toby Appel, in his book *The Cuvier-Geoffroy Debate: French Biology in the Decades Before Darwin* (Oxford: Oxford University Press, 1987), argues for the significant influence of the debate between Cuvier and Geoffroy on Darwin's attitude to morphology, as well as the mutual effect that the publication of *The Origin of Species* had on retrospective interest in the works of Cuvier and Geoffroy.
12. Georges Cuvier, *The Animal Kingdom* (London: Orr and Smith, 1834), pp. 25–6.
13. Continuing Aristotle's fundamental definition, see Elisabeth de Fontenay,

Le Silence des bêtes: La philosophie à l'épreuve de l'animalité (Paris: Fayard, 1998).

14. Cuvier, *The Animal Kingdom*, pp. 9–11.
15. Ibid., p. 22.
16. Ibid., p. 23.
17. Ibid.
18. Gould, *The Structure of Evolutionary Theory*, p. 296.
19. See Geoffroy Saint-Hilaire, *Philosophie Anatomique* (Paris: J.-B. Baillière, 1818).
20. Gould, *The Structure of Evolutionary Theory*, p. 300.
21. Ibid.
22. Bergson, *Creative Evolution*, p. 98.
23. Ibid., p. 112.
24. On this point, Bergson speculates on the place that fungi have in relation to this division of activity between plants and animals: 'It is a remarkable fact that the fungi, which nature has spread all over the earth in such extraordinary profusion, have not been able to evolve. Organically they do not rise above tissues which, in the higher vegetables, are formed in the embryonic sac of the ovary, and precede the germinative development of the new individual. They might be called the abortive children of the vegetable world. Their different species are like so many blind alleys, as if, by renouncing the mode of alimentation customary amongst vegetables, they had been brought to a standstill on the highway of vegetable evolution' (Bergson, *Creative Evolution*, p. 107).
25. Ibid., p. 101: 'But this would be only a manner of expression. There has been no particular impulse towards social life; there is simply the general movement of life, which on divergent lines is creating forms ever new.'
26. Ibid., p. 134.
27. Ibid., p. 135.
28. Ibid., p. 117.
29. Ibid., pp. 118–19.
30. August Weismann, *On Germinal Selection* (Chicago: The Open Court Publishing Company, 1902), p. 9.
31. Ibid., p. 5.
32. Ibid., p. 7.
33. Ibid., p. 26.
34. Ibid., p. 33.
35. Theodor Eimer, *On Orthogenesis and the Impotence of Natural Selection in Species-Formation* (Chicago: The Open Court Publishing Company, 1898), pp. 36–7.
36. Ibid., p. 56.
37. Ibid., p. 24; pp. 9–10.
38. Ibid., p. 36.
39. Eimer, *On Orthogenesis*, p. 33.
40. Bergson, *Creative Evolution*, p. 84.

41. Ibid., p. 41.
42. I will return, in detail, to the problem of mechanism versus organicism in Chapters 4 and 5. In particular, I will discuss how both Whitehead and Kauffman appeal to the very form of teleological organisation that Bergson rejects (internal finality), but also how they both reconfigure this concept to operate at all levels of organisation: at the level of individual organisms, but also at a sub-individual and supra-individual level.
43. Robert Tattersall and Benjamin Turner, 'Brown-Sequard and his Syndrome', *Lancet*, 356, 2000, pp. 61–3.
44. Bergson, *Creative Evolution*, p. 80. Brown-Séquard's eccentricities, as well as his innovations and contributions to neurology are documented by Michael J. Aminoff in 'Brown-Séquard and His Work on the Spinal Cord', *Spine*, 21:1, 1996, pp. 133–40. He notes that Brown-Séquard's experimental studies were conducted extensively not only on animals, but also on himself. In Chapter 6 I will discuss Donna Haraway's call for the practice of 'nonmimetic sharing' by scientists who use animals for research; whilst Brown-Séquard could not quite be credited with attempting to share the experiences of his test subjects in order to understand how to improve their conditions, he could at least be credited with the willingness to expose himself to levels of risk comparable to those inflicted on the animal subjects of his experiments.
45. Bergson, *Creative Evolution*, p. 79.
46. Ibid., p. 27.
47. Ibid., p. 55.
48. Ibid., p. 58.
49. Henri Bergson, *Mind-Energy: Lectures and Essays* (Westport, CT: Greenwood Press, 1975), p. 191.
50. Ibid., p. 192.
51. Ibid.
52. Ibid., pp. 194–5.
53. Ibid., pp. 197–8.
54. Ibid., p. 204.
55. Ibid., p. 210.
56. Ibid., p. 11.
57. Ibid., p. 13.
58. Ibid.
59. Ibid., p. 15
60. Ibid., p. 16.
61. Ibid., p. 22.
62. Ibid., p. 23.
63. Ibid., p. 24.
64. Ibid., p. 25.
65. Bergson, *Creative Evolution*, p. 60.
66. Stephen Jay Gould, *Wonderful Life: The Burgess Shale and the Nature of History* (London: Vintage, 2000), pp. 99–100.

67. Ibid., pp. 36–45.

68. See ibid., pp. 235–6. This recalls Bergson's comments about the retroactive nature of the concept of 'possibility': we have a tendency to derive what is possible from what we know to exist now. When we think about what *is* possible, we are actually thinking about what *was* possible. Using one of Gould's examples, we might take the many examples of trilobite fossils, traceable as far back as the Cambrian period as evidenced at Burgess, and conclude that the survival of that form was not only 'possible', but also, to some degree, necessary or inevitable.

69. Ibid., pp. 319–20.

70. Simon Conway Morris, *Life's Solution: Inevitable Humans in a Lonely Universe* (Cambridge University Press, 2003).

2. Pathological Life and the Limits of Medical Perception

... the knowledge of life, like the knowledge of society, assumes the priority of infraction over regularity.[1]

Georges Canguilhem's ascription of greater experimental value to the study of pathology over physiology (or normality), as propounded in his 1943 doctoral thesis in medicine, *The Normal and the Pathological* (expanded and republished in 1966), is not simply a description of the limits of medical perception. It is also a philosophical statement about the nature of life as a 'struggle against that which obstructs its preservation and development taken as norms',[2] and the nature of life's knowledge of itself: 'Disease is the source of the speculative attention which life attaches to life by means of man.'[3]

This interrelation between the knowledge of life and analysis of the diseased state of the living organism recalls and problematises Henri Bergson's analysis in *Creative Evolution* of the progressive adaptation of human intellect and matter in the evolution of human intelligence.[4] Bergson's aim was to explain the propensity of the human intellect, and the development of its activity in the sciences, to attach itself to artificial, stable forms over against the real, moving continuity of vital and material processes. In these terms, it would be necessary to resist the normal direction of thought in order to achieve an understanding of the living. However, this would pose difficulties for Bergson's critics and proponents alike in his apparent perpetuation of the gulf between the arts and the sciences: since Bergson could be dismissed as anti-scientific and subjectivist, his critics would be left unable to illuminate this thought except by crude generalisations about its place in the history of philosophy,[5] and his proponents unable to participate in discussions on the history and philosophy of science except to malign the sciences for their insufficiencies in accounting for real change or living processes. One of the intentions of the previous chapter was to cast light on the reality of Bergson's attitude towards the sciences, one that is certainly not dismissive, and on the contrary seeks to establish a more productive relationship between philosophy and the sciences by discovering their common origins, pitfalls, and potential for shared endeavours in problem-solving.

Resisting a straightforward dismissal of Bergson's perspective on the problem of the separation of life from scientific analysis, Canguilhem's approach recognises the diseased state as integral to the character of living matter, and highlights the need for medicine and its associated areas of study (anatomy, physiology, histology, embryology, etc.) to be treated in isolation from the wider fields of the physical sciences (physics, biology), because only the former manifest polarities between normal and pathological activity: 'When the wastes of digestion are no longer excreted by the organism and congest or poison the internal environment, this is all indeed according to law (physical, chemical, etc.) but none of this follows the norm, which is the activity of the organism itself.'[6] That is, Canguilhem propounds the idea that there are no objective norms in the physical sciences, and therefore no states that are equivalent to the pathological states of living bodies. In this way, he accentuates the specialised activity of medical investigation: pathology is taken as life's unique, internal problematic and it is therefore only through the study of disease that we are able to discern the 'normal' functions of life.

The aim of this chapter is to examine Henri Bergson's response to the *medical* articulation of living processes. In particular it will focus on Bergson's theories of perception, image and 'attention to life' in his 1896 work *Matter and Memory* in the light of Michel Foucault's analysis (in *The Birth of the Clinic*) of the concepts of life and death that emerged from certain developments in the medical sciences in the early nineteenth century. I will begin with Foucault's assessment of Bergson's predecessors in the fields of medical and bio-scientific investigation, in particular Xavier Bichat. In *The Birth of the Clinic*, Foucault shows how Bichat's methods contributed to the progression of medicine towards positivism in so far as it dispensed with speculations on the vital principle in favour of the centrality accorded to the body at the point of death. Foucault's analysis will echo and take further the analyses of Canguilhem of the priority of disease in the study of physiological states. I will then turn to some of the key insights of Claude Bernard set out in his *Introduction to Experimental Medicine*, and follow with an analysis of Bergson's *Matter and Memory* which incorporates a critique of medical investigation in response to nineteenth-century physiology.

This 'critique' consists in uncovering a number of underlying metaphysical assumptions about the relations between mind and body and between mind and world. Finally, I will argue that Bergson's *Matter and Memory* can thus be understood as a response to the problem of the centrality of death in medical investigation. It is precisely the banishment of lived time to the realm of empty metaphysical speculation that simply reinforces the status that Kantianism had accorded metaphysics in opposition to the natural sciences. For Bergson, the separation between thought and object instituted by the Kantian scheme would be tackled through their unification in a theory of images. In these terms, it would be necessary to recognise the integral impurity of perception by virtue of the continuous (conscious and unconscious) operation of memory in all conscious activity, including scientific or medical perception, and thus to acknowledge the effect that different perceptual modes may have on our capacity to understand living processes.

LIFE, DEATH AND MEDICINE

In his 1963 work, *The Birth of the Clinic*, Michel Foucault would take further Canguilhem's prioritisation of disease in his historical analysis of the emergence of clinical medicine in the nineteenth century as concomitant with the migration of the concept of death to the centre of an understanding of life. At issue for Foucault are a number of received ideas about the conditions of possibility of medical advancement in this era, in particular the assumption that society had experienced an enlightened movement away from the prohibition on the use of corpses for study to an acceptance of the necessity of autopsy. Rather, as Foucault would go on to argue, the very concepts of knowledge and its limits, life and death, would participate in a 'syntactical reorganisation of disease in which the limits of the visible and invisible follow a new pattern'.[7]

From Bergson to Canguilhem and Foucault, there is a sustained engagement with the interconnectedness of the concept of life, the forms of visibility, and the question of the proper object of scientific analysis. In Martin Jay's study *Downcast Eyes: The Denigration of Vision in Twentieth-Century French Thought*, these and many other French philosophical and literary figures are placed on the same 'anti-visual' (anti-representational) trajectory, in reaction to 'the domination of the ancient scopic regime' or Cartesian perspectivalism.[8] Included in Jay's reading is a clear lineage drawn from Bergson to Foucault on the basis of their shared rejection of visually biased and representational models of thought, despite their usual characterisation as opposing philosophical figures (typically, in terms of Bergson's continuism as against Foucault's thinking of discontinuity, after Bachelard and Canguilhem).

Foucault's *The Birth of the Clinic* is commonly cited together with his earlier work, *Madness and Civilization* (1961) for its continuation of an engagement with the impact of Phillippe Pinel's medical practices and classification of diseases across the eighteenth and nineteenth centuries. In *The Birth of the Clinic* this continuation would take place in the context of the interactions between Pinel's work and the writings and experimental methods of Xavier Bichat.[9] Foucault's study sets out a number of events and factors that had contributed to the rise of a particular configuration of clinical medicine in the nineteenth century[10] that persists today, in particular the incorporation of a concept of death within medical theory, no longer simply as a negative value (the absence of life) but as the concrete basis of the study of living processes.

The often noted divergence between the work of Foucault and Bergson, largely based on the opposition between space and time, takes for granted the potency of some inherited tendencies in the history of recent French thought. In a defence of the continued value of Bergson's philosophical method within the trajectory of French epistemology, Elie During quotes a number of the typical 'overdeterminations' of the influence of Bergsonism (whether positive or 'reactive', from Merleau-Ponty, to Deleuze and Foucault). Foucault himself is attributed some share of the responsibility for perpetuating a reaction against Bergson's valorisation of time over space. However, During rightly qualifies this by pointing out that

> Foucault's reference to 'a Bergsonian valorisation of time' does not only function as a philosophical cliché. It may in fact best be explained from an auto-biographical perspective. It is with the academic primacy of Bergsonian time (or Bergsonian primacy of time) that Foucault himself had to struggle in the fifties and sixties, as he tried to foster a new form of investigation invested in the constructions of space – sites, boundaries, thresholds, where power inscribes its marks.[11]

In his own words, in setting out his 'archaeological' project, Foucault distances himself from participating in the kinds of oppositional thinking that simply repeat Bachelard's prioritisation of discontinuity in reaction to Bergsonian *durée*:

> It is understandable that some minds are so attached to all those old metaphors by which, for a century and a half, history (movement, flux, evolution) has been imagined, that they see archaeology simply as the negation of history and the crude affirmation of discontinuity; the truth is that they cannot accept that change should be cleansed of all these adventitious

models, that it should be deprived of both its primacy as a universal law and its status as a general effect, and that it should be replaced by the analysis of various transformations.[12]

The way in which Foucault, in *The Archaeology of Knowledge*, goes on to reinforce the aim of *The Birth of the Clinic* principally in terms of shifts in medical language (e.g. from classificatory to statistical), means that key concepts of body, organ, disease, life and death are subjected to a reorganisation *secondary to* wider social and political shifts in the settings of medical practice and the boundaries of medical perception. As Foucault writes:

> In *Naissance de la clinique*, the essential point of the research was the way in which, at the end of the eighteenth and the beginning of the nineteenth century, the enunciative forms of medical discourse had been modified; the analysis was concerned therefore less with the formation of conceptual systems, or the formation of theoretical choices, than with the status, the institutional siting, the situation, and the modes of insertion used by the discoursing subject.[13]

Again, Foucault distances himself from any portrayal of the totalising, imperious gaze of the physician, which might be suggested by his term *regard médical*: 'In the proposed analysis, instead of referring back to *the* synthesis or *the* unifying function of *a* subject, the various enunciative modalities manifest his dispersion.'[14] Here, Foucault's focus on space and spatialisation in historical analysis is indeed a reaction to the predominance of Bergsonian thought in the study of philosophy in France in the twentieth century, and it is thus also a defence and development of what is essentially the most 'anti-visual' strand of Bergsonism. It would therefore be an oversimplification to cite the two thinkers within the same anti-visual trajectory, if the critique of spatialised thought is taken to be the core of Bergson's reaction to the primacy of visual models. Rather, Foucault, like Bergson, works in confrontation with the Kantian subjective model by providing alternative explanations for the persistence of certain structures in human thought, without attributing those structures to thought inherently.

THE LEGACY OF XAVIER BICHAT

Foucault's study of the conceptual and methodological shifts in medical thought that took place in the nineteenth century summarises the shifts in primacy of two main ways of categorising disease: nosology and pathological anatomy. A narrative about the changing relationship between the two forms of study is constructed around the

predominantly *spatial* character of the classificatory method of nosology ('the flat surface of perpetual simultaneity. Table and picture'[15]),
for which 'the time of the body does not affect, and still less determines, the time of the disease',[16] and the linear, *temporal* progression
of symptoms of the diseased body as studied from the point of view of
pathological anatomy.

Some suggestions about the consequences of reconciling these two
positions are provided through the work of Xavier Bichat and a number
of his contemporaries, in the fields of anatomy and physiology in particular. Bichat's basic definition of life in his *Physiological Researches
on Life and Death* (published in 1800) places death at the centre of life
and, consequently, shows disease to be the principal indicator of vital
activity: 'The definition of life is usually sought for in abstract consid-
erations; it will be found, if I mistake not, in the following expression:
Life consists in the sum of the functions, by which death is resisted.'[17]
The incorporation of death into a transformed understanding of the
body's relation to disease is not attributable, Foucault argues, to a
sudden 'enlightened' acceptance of the dissection of corpses. Rather,
it merely reflects a shift in understanding of the point at which death
begins, exemplified by Bichat's account of the many 'partial deaths'
that occur in natural death, a process commencing with the shutting
down of functions that characterise 'animal life' (sensory, cerebral
and motor functions that underpin voluntary activity), followed by
the 'organic' functions that mark the body's affectivity (or its physico-
chemical reactivity).[18] This extension of the duration of death, and thus
its encroachment upon the time of the living body, is accompanied by
a reconfiguration of corporeal space itself. Bichat's innovation in mem-
brane analysis (generally held to be the precursor of modern histology),
in which the distinction between the internal functions of organs and
their external effects is dissolved in favour of a readable membranous
surface, enacts this spatialisation of the diseased body: 'Between the
tissues and the systems the organs appear as simple functional folds,
entirely relative, both in their role and in their disorders, to the elements
of which they are made up and to the groups to which they belong.'[19]

Thus the development of the 'anatomo-clinical method' is characterised by a unification from the point of view of death (the cadaver) of
'lesional occurrences' or the condition of the organs at death, observations of the signs of disease in progress (particular tissue types display-
ing particular forms of degeneration), and a probabilistic analysis of
different cases of the same or similar diseases. This unification overcomes any notion of disease attacking life, and yields instead a concept
of *pathological life*:

Spatialised in the organism in accordance with their own lines and areas, pathological phenomena take on the appearance of living processes. This has two consequences: disease is hooked onto life itself, feeding on it . . . It is no longer an event or a nature imported from the outside; it is life undergoing modification in an inflected functioning.[20]

Overall, this new method represents a significant shift in the *language* and the *space* or readable surface of the living body. Here, the relationship between life and death, as correlates of visibility and invisibility, is reversed. For example, the associations between life, ideality and what is knowable, against death, materiality and the unknowable are reversed in Bichat's rejection of metaphysical speculations on the source or animating principle of life:

To seek the connexion of first causes with their general effects is to walk blindfold in a road from whence a thousand paths diverge. Of what importance besides to us are these causes? Is it necessary to know the nature of light, of oxygen and caloric to study their phenomena? Without the knowledge of the principle of life, cannot we analyse its properties? In the study of animals let us proceed as modern metaphysicians have done in that of the understanding. Let us suppose causes, and attach ourselves to their general results.[21]

It is worth pointing out here Bichat's generally accepted association with vitalism. For example, Canguilhem, in his essay 'Cell Theory', argues that Bichat's work on membranes is grounded on an adherence to the idea of the continuity of living matter: 'Seen by Bichat to be the fabric out of which living beings are cut, tissue offers an image adequate to the continuity of the vital fact, as required by vitalist exigency.'[22] Opposed to this membranous continuity would be the individuation or discontinuity of the cell, taken to be the most rudimentary components of any living organism.

In Foucault's account of Bichat's role in the development of clinical medicine, the omission of an underlying metaphysical unity is not then portrayed as a retreat into a mechanistic view of corporeality, but as the introduction of a new 'mortalism': death is the historical a priori of the clinic, in so far as it signals medicine's firm alignment with materialism and the absolute visibility of the body. If we agree with Foucault that a hierarchisation of mortality over vitality amounts to at least a subtle break with the vitalistic interpretation of the functions of the body, then Bichat's descriptive focus on the organic orientation around and towards death can be seen as essentially positivist in character. On this view, it is Bergson's philosophy that would later remain as the representative of the old vitalist regime according to which corporeal life owes its complexity to a spiritual (temporal) aspect of its being.[23]

Until that point, Bichat's impact had been to reinforce the experimental focus on disease as indicator of the body's natural or accidental journey towards death, which in turn meant that medicine had become the art of managing pathological life, perceiving life from the perspective of its efforts to avoid and overcome disease.

BERNARD AND BERGSON: THE STUDY OF LIFE AND THE STUDY OF THOUGHT

In the following section, I will turn to two essays by Bergson: (i) 'Psycho-Physical Parallelism and Positive Metaphysics', originally published in 1901, and formed in part in response to criticisms to some of the main theses of Bergson's 1896 work *Matter and Memory*; and (ii) 'The Philosophy of Claude Bernard' (1913) that appears in English translation in *The Creative Mind* (originally published in France in 1934). Some of Bergson's claims in these two essays provide insights into the relation between the aims of *Matter and Memory* and the development and focus of the medical sciences in the nineteenth century that I have just discussed.

First of all, in 'Psycho-Physical Parallelism and Positive Metaphysics', Bergson's discussion refers us to a definition of conscious or active life as 'an immense effort made by thought to obtain something from matter that matter does not want to give up'.[24] In this definition, Bergson is essentially making reference to one of the central claims of *Matter and Memory* that mind's effort to release matter from its inertial state leads us to a theory of perception that is primarily oriented towards useful action. The other aspect of this claim is that the degrees of freedom of a living being's actions are determined by variations in the interposition of memories upon those actions. Now, whereas the efficacy of any action can be measured (and documented through experiment) independently of the operation of consciousness, since activity motivated by the most rudimentary kinds of 'memory', i.e., habit and instinct, can be extremely effective and efficient, it is the *choice* exercised in an action that tends to elude measurement. Bergson argues this repeatedly, with different emphases, and in relation to different branches of the sciences of 'life', across a number of his main works (i.e., *Time and Free Will*, *Matter and Memory*, *Creative Evolution*, *The Two Sources of Morality and Religion*). The common theme across these works is the focus on the potential for philosophy to provide alternative but complementary perspectives on key problems in the life sciences (psychology, neuro-physiology, evolutionary biology and social anthropology, respectively), particularly with regard to their own definitions of 'life' and how this determines their methods for studying living processes.

Now, the problem of psycho-physical parallelism, which as a modern psychological problem does not seem to be making a particularly strong or interesting claim (although it does reflect, for example, the Leibnizian and Spinozist theories of universal mechanism where mind and body say the same thing in different languages[25]), is significant for Bergson because it shows how the relationship between 'thinking man' and the living being (the metaphysical and physical) has, historically, been described inadequately.[26] Bergson is interested less in defending the 'old spiritualist' claim that the mind cannot be reduced to matter, and more in asking the question 'to what extent?'[27] That is, he is interested in determining the limitations on our ability to think about the relation between mental/psychological and physical/cerebral states (hence, the extended discussion on mind/body dualism in *Matter and Memory*). His ambition for philosophy is thus set out as follows:

> A metaphysics that began by moulding itself around the contour of such facts would have many of the characteristics of an undisputed science. And it would be open to an indefinite progress, because the increasingly precise determination of the relation of consciousness to its material conditions, by showing us with growing accuracy on what points, and in which directions, and by which necessities our thought is limited, would guide us in the very special effort that we have to make to free ourselves of this limitation.[28]

In his essay on Claude Bernard, Bergson points out two main features of Bernard's work with which he has a particular affinity, and that provide an insight into what Bergson sees as the correct approach to understanding the relation between mental and physical states. The first of Bernard's main claims is that physiology, despite the difficulties associated with describing living processes, deserves to be a deterministic science. Bernard does acknowledge the vagueness of the concept of life, as exemplified in statements such as the following from his *Introduction to the Study of Experimental Medicine* (1865): 'we must always seek to exclude life entirely from our explanations of physiological phenomena as a whole. Life is nothing but a word which means ignorance, and when we characterise a phenomenon as vital, it amounts to saying that we do not know its immediate cause or its conditions.'[29] However, this is not an obstacle to Bergson's admiration for Bernard's work, since it belies the significance that Bernard accords to physiology as a distinct science.[30] Canguilhem, incidentally, criticises Bernard for his theory that pathological states are merely greater or lesser intensities of normal states.[31] Instead, Canguilhem supports the thesis that the pathological state is discontinuous with the physiological (normal) state; hence, pathology is the principal science involving the application of surgical and medical technology to derive knowledge about physiological states negatively. Life in its 'normal' functioning is practically imperceptible, and only makes itself visible in disease and death.

A key implication of Bernard's statements in his *Introduction to the Study of Experimental Medicine* is the need for science to recognise its own limitations. In engaging in the attempt to formulate a deterministic science of physiology, Bernard emphasises the restriction of scientific study to the determination of 'the conditions of phenomena', which specifically entails the rejection of any appeal to a vital principle: 'Vital force is an organising and nutritive force; but it does not in any way determine the manifestation of the properties of living matter. In a word, physiologists and physicians must seek to reduce vital properties to physico-chemical properties, and not physico-chemical properties to vital properties.'[32] Despite these statements, Bergson sees Bernard's search for a rigorous science of physiology as a recognition of the importance of the concept of life and the question of its most appropriate method of study, both of which are in keeping with Bergson's own philosophical preoccupations.[33]

The second significant aspect of Bernard's work is the claim that scientific method (and, for Bergson, what constitutes Bernard's 'philosophy') should be flexible and unsystematic. As Bernard observes:

> Experimental medicine, like all the experimental sciences, should not go beyond phenomena, it does not need to be tied to any system; it is neither vitalistic, nor animistic, nor organistic, nor solidistic, nor humoral; it is simply the science which tries to reach the immediate causes of vital phenomena in the healthy and in the morbid state. It has no reason, in fact, to encumber itself with systems, none of which can ever embody the truth.[34]

For Bergson, the value of Bernard's work lies in this methodological project, an essential part of which is the rejection of ideas and theories once they are found to be inadequate to the phenomena being described: 'An idea, no matter how flexible we may have made it, will never have the same flexibility as a thing. Let us therefore be ready to abandon it for another, which will fit the experiment still more closely.'[35] On this view, 'remaining faithful to a method involves constantly remodelling its form on the basis of its subject, in order to maintain the same precision of fit.'[36] In *Matter and Memory*, Bergson's adoption of Bernard's methodology is manifested in his attempt to overcome philosophical dualisms, in this instance mind and body (or matter), where, he argues, important insights into their functioning can be gained by considering the point at which the two terms meet, 'at their common frontier, in order to study the form and nature of their contact'.[37] In the next section, I will examine how Bergson sets about this exploration of the 'common frontier' of mind and matter.

BERGSON'S *MATTER AND MEMORY*: THE SCIENCES AND MIND/BODY DUALISM

At the core of Bergson's critique of psychological approaches to brain disorders in *Matter and Memory* is a wider criticism of empirical analysis, its error being that it 'substitutes for true experience, that experience which arises from the immediate contact of the mind with its object, an experience which is disarticulated and, therefore, most probably, disfigured – at any rate arranged for the greater facility of action and of language'.[38] This criticism constitutes an attack on the parallelism of mental and cerebral states and, therefore, on a direct relation between perception and pure knowledge, since what is scientifically observable constitutes only the part of mental activity that is 'capable of translating itself into movements of locomotion'.[39] Bergson characteristically attributes the same postulate, in this case that 'to perceive means to know', to both idealism for which science is a symbolic expression of the real, and realism, for which perception is a confused and provisional science.[40] The primary orientation of perception towards action is affirmed, first of all, in terms of the presence in the totality of organic life of all degrees of involuntary, instinctive behaviour, and voluntary action; this demonstrates the principal function of the nervous system which is to 'receive stimulation, to provide motor apparatus, and to present the largest possible number of these apparatuses to a given stimulus'.[41] Secondly, it is affirmed in the subordination of representation to the process of acquiring a greater, or more indeterminate, facility for action.

In turning to the field of psychology itself in his 1910 introduction to *Matter and Memory*, Bergson reiterates the need to place action, rather than knowledge, at the centre of psychic life:

> That which is commonly held to be a disturbance of the psychic life itself, an inward disorder, a disease of the personality, appears to us, from our point of view, to be an unloosing or a breaking of the tie which binds this psychic life to its motor accompaniment, a weakening or an impairing of our attention to outward life. This opinion, as also that which denies the localisation of the memory-images of words and explains aphasia quite otherwise than by such localisation, was considered paradoxical at the date of the first publication of the present work (1896). It will appear much less so now.[42]

The analysis of contemporary psychological theories of memory and the brain and Bergson's own development of a theory of memory raises a number of problems that have, as Bergson points out, a particular meta-physical significance. One of these problems as set out in Chapter 4 of *Matter and Memory* is that of 'the union of soul and body', the analysis of which attempts to explain how there is (a) a profound *distinction* between matter and 'spirit', as well as (b) a *union* between them.[43] Posing these questions allows for the extension of the analyses of the preceding chapters, on the nature and function of the body in relation to memory, to also include some thoughts on 'Nature' (or the material universe) itself. Bergson's approach to this task involves a confrontation with a set of received dualisms underlying certain materialist and idealist doctrines that have determined the parameters of the mind/body problem.

The inextension of mind (of perceptions), on the one hand, and the extensity of matter (of perceived objects), on the other, are usually 'rec-onciled' either by deriving mind from matter (materialism) or by making matter the construction of mind (idealism). The essential point, for Bergson, is that both doctrines avoid an appreciation of the difference *in kind* between the opposing terms by attributing reality to just one of them. In *Matter and Memory*, the objective is to accord a real existence to both matter and mind, instead of rendering them mutually exclusive. Thus, in the case of idealism,[44] Bergson attacks the assumption that the 'understanding designs the plan of nature', by describing it instead 'as a certain faculty of dissociating, of distinguishing, of opposing logically, but not of creating or of constructing'.[45] Against materialism, Bergson asserts the independence of representations ('images') from cerebral matter. Crucially in this text Bergson's first aim concerning memory is to establish its *selective* function, affirming at the same time the *distinc-tion* between mind's representations and matter. However, the ques-tion of the *union* or 'continuity' of mind and matter rests on Bergson's conception of Time in its relation to 'Duration' and 'Memory'. The true reconciliation of mind and matter (that is, the explanation of their possible interaction) takes place with the attenuation of the oppositions between the unextended (perceptions) and the extended (matter), and between qualities (the heterogeneity of sensations in consciousness) and quantities (the homogeneity of movements in space). Now whereas the first opposition would be 'resolved' in the theory of pure perception contained in the first chapter of *Matter and Memory*, Bergson refers to his theory of pure memory as the principle by which quantity becomes the relative 'dilution' of quality for the greater facility of action and retrospective analysis.

The various theories that Bergson attacks (realism, idealism, mate-rialism, etc.) apportion to either matter or mind the greater share in reality. Bergson, in his defence of the 'reality of spirit' (indicated by the preservation or endurance of memories independently of the brain), is tackling this point when he highlights the tendency in both psychology and philosophy to accord to unperceived objects (outside the mind) an independent reality (e.g. an unoccupied room). Yet at the same time this is also the tendency to deny the possibility of images that are no longer present to consciousness, that is, memories no longer relevant to the present situation or action, being existent in an *un*conscious form. The way in which Bergson confronts this tendency involves a recasting of the definition and role of consciousness in experience as a whole. The new role granted to consciousness is achieved through an extension of the definition of 'existence' (for us). According to Bergson, our apprehensions of internal 'psychical' states are primarily thought to 'exist' only when present to consciousness, and external physical objects primarily 'exist' for us as a series of regularly or causally connected elements. Bergson's theory of duration, or of the fundamental coexistence of the past in the present, arises from the need to address the problems raised by apportioning to mind and matter only one of the two ways of existing. Such a move, Bergson claims, has led to the separation of mind and matter according to a clear-cut distinction that results in a theory of mind in which conscious/mental states are completely transparent or readable in a present action, and a theory of matter that is 'mysterious' except for its conformity to laws of succession: 'The material object, just because of the multitude of unperceived elements by which it is linked with all other objects, appears to enfold within itself and to hide behind it infinitely more than it allows to be seen.'[46] In other words, the association between existence and succession in the case of matter is resolved into a conception of matter synonymous with its spatial and geometrical determinations (the dominance of space precluding a real or effective time); and the association between existence and presence to consciousness precludes any theory of *unconscious* mental states, which restricts psychological theories to the reconstruction of mental activity from a series of 'present' states. This latter emphasis on 'presence' is achieved through the denial of any temporal/causal connection between those mental states.[47] Bergson's account exposes the way in which an incommensurable gap between matter and mind is instituted, thereby giving rise to the problem of how mind and matter are able to interact.

IMAGES AND THE IMPURE GAZE: THE MEANING OF ATTENTION TO LIFE

In the remainder of this chapter I will discuss how Bergson attempts to reconcile our understanding of mental and material states in terms of a theory of images. As we will see, Bergson's recourse to a theory of images constitutes an attempt to overcome the opposition instituted by Kantianism between things in themselves and representations. What Bergson's analysis accentuates is the role of the *reflections* of object-images onto one another, expressing the variability in intensity of action in the attention to life of the perceiving and acting subject, often, Bergson explains, more visible in cases of neuro-pathology:

> By converging lines of facts, by the facts of normal recognition, by the facts of pathological recognition, by mental [psychic] blindness in particular, and finally and above all by the various forms of sensory aphasia, I was led to the conclusion that the brain contains 'motor schemas' of images and ideas, that at every instant it traces out their motor articulations, which, as a result and to a certain extent and in certain ways, condition thought.[48]

The physical or cerebral state (the motor schemas) will be shown to be only a small part of the whole of thought and action, confronting the problem of perception that has historically been conceived in terms of the structure of the perceiving organ, principally the eye. As F. C. T. Moore explains:

> An Aristotelian view of perception, which has persisted up to now, was that an adequate account should be derivable from a study of the intrinsic properties of the organ of perception and of its interaction with the environment. This would make pure perception a primarily biological phenomenon. But there is a serious limitation to this view, however attractive it may at first seem, and whatever important truth it contains. For what we *in fact* perceive is not determined solely by the physiological factors which determine what we are *capable of* discriminating. It is necessary in addition to take account of what we want or need to perceive, and of how we learn to perceive in one way rather than another.[49]

Félix Ravaisson, for example, puts forward just such an analysis of the effects of our physical perceptual apparatus on representations of perspective in painting, in his discussion of Leonardo da Vinci's diagrams of the operations of the eye, in which there is a condensation of the whole perceptual field onto the small surface of the retina, which in turn gives rise to our perception of converging lines at the furthest point of the horizon in the visual field.[50] This appreciation, at a physical level, of the distorting nature of perception, prefigures in some respects Bergson's cone diagram in *Matter and Memory*, featuring the varying concentrations of different levels of memory and the 'deeper strata of reality' onto the interlinking virtual and actual images at the plane of action. Taken together, an (Aristotelian) appeal to the organic structure of the eye itself, the physical reflection of light between objects, and the concomitant distortion (contraction) of real objects on the visual plane (discussed in Ravaisson's essay on da Vinci) develops in Bergson's work into an epistemological account of the effects of the variation in degrees of 'attention to life' on our perception and action upon objects. Bergson accentuates the way in which 'every *attentive* perception truly involves a *reflection*, in the etymological sense of the word, that is to say the projection, outside ourselves, of an actively created image, identical with, or similar to, the object on which it comes to mould itself'.[51]

In this analysis, Bergson further explores how perception is both distinct from and tied to life, in so far as there is no conscious perception without the infiltration of memory, which is the temporal dimension of subjectivity. In order to understand the body and its functions, psychology would need to consider this temporal/vital aspect. Instead, it mistakes present moments for its object of study and builds an entire scientific endeavour upon a theory of physical, cerebral, 'stored' memories, when in fact they are merely instantaneous sections carved out of the 'stream of becoming'. On one side, Bergson exposes the philosophical assumptions underlying the seemingly pure and positive approaches of psychology, and on the other he suggests a reconfiguration of the relation between matter or nature and the perception of it in terms of a theory of memory or duration. The aim is to avoid the explanation of perception in terms of a purely physical elision of matter and mind (as the cerebral storage of memories does). Instead, the intention is to provide a theory that explains not only the real distinction between perception and memory, but also their possible interaction.

The theory of images in *Matter and Memory* thus returns to one of the fundamental problems which Kantian transcendental subjectivity had attempted to solve. Against the idealist position (for which an object can only be a representation for us) and the materialist position (for which an object is an independently existing thing), Bergson provides a description of a world of matter defined as an aggregate of images, and the perception of that matter as '*these same images referred to the eventual action of one particular image, my body*'.[52] Importantly, the organisation of images around the central image of the body entails a selection or subtraction of what is irrelevant to its impending action:

> [A body] does not react to all properties; it need not represent any property; but it does tend to respond to the properties important to it. This is why *representation* is a bad picture of perception. Perceiving, in a living body, is not making a picture of an object, but selecting just some of its properties in the light of that body's needs and projects, of what Bergson calls its *virtual actions*.[53]

In invoking 'images', as the grounding units of the material world, Bergson aims to unite ontological and epistemological accounts of objectivity, by integrating an object's appearance into the definition of its very existence: 'For common sense, then, the object exists in itself, and, on the other hand, the object is, in itself, pictorial, as we perceive it: image it is, but a self-existing image.'[54]

Bergson puts forward an account of the world populated by beings of greater or lesser powers of acting, distinguished in this way by their own rhythms of duration, and which measure 'the degree of tension or relaxation of different kinds of consciousness and thereby fix their respective places in the scale of being'.[55] In this material universe conceived as a system of inter-linked images, living matter is distinguished by its tendency to form centres of real action (the body as central image), which are the variations in capacity of some of these images to affect surrounding objects/images. In Bergson's terminology, these variations describe the relative distance between virtual action (or virtual objectivity composed of memory-images) and real action (composed of perception-images). Furthermore, these different levels of capacity to act are, for example, indicated by the variations in complexity of the perceptual apparatuses of different organisms.[56] Commencing at the most basic relation between perceiver and perceived, the account of 'real action' that Bergson provides expresses the highest degree of 'attention to life' which is immediate contact and action, as opposed to 'dream' or inattention where memory-images are unfocused and are yet to be selected for the purpose of active contact with objects. The formation of subjectivity articulated in terms of a body's tendency to act is, at this primitive level, also the tendency of surrounding objects to reflect the body's capacity to act upon them:

> The more I narrow this horizon, the more the objects which it circumscribes space themselves out distinctly according to the greater or lesser ease with which my body can touch and move them. They send back, then, to my body, as would a mirror, its eventual influence; they take rank in an order corresponding to the growing or decreasing powers of my body.[57]

This relation between acting body and acted-upon objects describes the operation of both habit (automatic actions acquired through repetition) and instinct (genetically inherited automatic reactions) in living organisms. Instinct, for example, expresses the capacity of an organism to affect its environment through the inscription on the body itself of motor action as a heritable physiological characteristic. In this way the gap between action and object is as small as possible, and the intervention of memory (understood separately from this physical 'memory' of instinctual action) is negligible. Similarly, the process of acquiring a habit terminates in the appearance (that is, *imitation*) of an instinctive action, and again relies on nothing more than a superficial (anatomical and physiological) 'mirroring' of the body and the objects it acts upon.[58]

Now, recall that on one hand the psychological approach denies the temporal reality of memory by focusing only on the habit-forming and instinctive aspects of memory which are readable in present actions. This would necessarily make the brain and nervous system the appropriate focus for psychological study. On the other hand, it reduces perception to affectivity or the collection of sensory data subjectively experienced, thereby denying the real and independent existence of objects:

> Because sensation (on account of the *confused* effort which it involves) is only vaguely localised, [the psychologist] declares it unextended, and thence makes sensation in general the simple element from which we obtain by composition all external images. The truth is that affection is not the primary matter of which perception is made; it is rather the impurity with which perception is alloyed.[59]

As we saw above, the basic operations of instinctive and habitual action involved sensory-perceptual experience without the intervention of consciousness. For Bergson, memory should only be implicated in the introduction of an element of choice or freedom to our actions. This true memory, as the temporal dimension (duration) of perceptual experience, is expressed in the form of virtual objectivity:

> Our perception of an object distinct from our body, separated from our body by an interval, never expresses anything but a *virtual* action. But the more distance decreases between this object and our body (the more, in other words, the danger becomes urgent or the promise immediate), the more does virtual action tend to pass into *real* action. Suppose the distance reduced to zero, that is to say that the object to be perceived coincides with our body, that is to say again, that our body is the object to be perceived. Then it is no longer virtual action, but real action, that this specialised perception will express, and this is exactly what affection is.[60]

What emerges is a refined definition of 'representation' that expresses a combination of objects themselves and their external relation to a body's potential to act upon them. This representation belongs to the realm of instinct and habit in so far as it comes to replace conscious or newly created actions over time. Living matter (organic body, centre of real action), described in this way as a privileged image among many other images, with varying levels of power to act on other images, gives us a theory focused upon the body only when it is engaged in *the process of acting*; whereas the psychological approach criticised by Bergson mistakes the nervous system's orientation towards action for the whole of consciousness. Overall, then, Bergson attributes the shortcomings of a scientific (i.e., positivist and 'ocularcentric') explanation of memory based on habit to a failure to recognise the flexibility that differing degrees of 'attention to life' allow in the operation of virtual objectivity, or the projection of our varying power to act on surrounding objects. The 'spatialising' tendency of perception (for the purposes of utility) is revealed to be only one aspect of our conscious operations, and, by extension, scientific thought must not be rejected but rather subjected to critique and refined – become flexible and unsystematic, as Claude Bernard argues – in order for it to become adequate to the task of understanding life.

Let us return, then, to Foucault, in *The Birth of the Clinic*, in which he proceeded with a double spatialisation: first, in terms of his method for analysing the ascendancy of clinical medicine, i.e., as the conjunction of a number of social, economic and judiciary factors that favoured particular medical practices; second, in an alternative conception of the space of the body in terms of tissue/membranes. This would result in the promotion of a language of membranes or pure surfaces in different stages of degradation and reactivity, rather than the action of an external agent (disease) on the body's organic unity: the body's diseases became the signs of its progress towards death. This marked the shift in medicine from a relation of the integral health of the body and the external threat of disease to one of the normal and pathological states of the body from the point of view of Death. While Foucault's analysis illuminates the conjunction of factors that gave rise to this new view of the relation between life and death, and indeed to the centrality of death and an understanding of the morbid states of the body in the advancement of medical science, in turning to Bergson's responses to nineteenth-century medical thought, the tendencies and limitations of medical perception, as an extension of ordinary perception, are revealed to be an equally important factor in shaping our understanding of the living organism. P. A. Y. Gunter's arguments for the consideration of Bergsonian thought as a basis for environmentalism also suggest two key contributions that Bergson's philosophy makes to our thinking of the vital in general.[61] Bergson's theory of knowledge is both accepting of the advance of science and technology but also willing to submit them to critique, in particular for their limitations or inherently (though not always acknowledged) perspectival analytical schemes: 'Why not appeal to intuition, not as a perception by the mind of the "self-evidence" of some sort of truth, but as a participation in the processes of things? One would then at least have the hope of escaping conceptual structures founded essentially on the need to control and reshape our world.'[62] This re-shaping of our world, from the point of view of environmentalism, is one aspect of our 'war against nature', and Bergson's analysis of the conditions of concrete experience, in the utility-driven operations of ordinary perception, constitute a first step in re-orienting human life in relation to the rest of the natural world. Taken together with Bergson's approach to the concept of evolution – in a move echoed in Jung's concept of a racial unconscious – he proposes that human beings have 'a biological unconscious: a reminiscence of all the "vague potentialities" inherent in life' – a renewed attitude to scientific advancement and our place in nature suggests the possibility, available to all of us, of fostering 'a sympathy with all living things'.[63]

We have here a statement of a fundamental insufficiency or tendency in the development of scientific thought, one that has its basis in the tendencies of ordinary consciousness, that is, in the propensity to think or determine things, including other animals, in terms of their relative utility. Medical perception, as an extension of the biological sciences, is unavoidably distorting. It carries with it the risk of reducing life to disease and death even though, as we have seen, what this reduction engendered was an invigoration of the study of biological processes for the benefit of our understanding of morbidity within human populations. The concept of pathological life thus played a certain role in sharpening our ability to see, to understand, the living organism at the very limit of its functions and capacities. I want to go on to demonstrate, commencing in the next chapter, that thinking life in terms of pathology, exception and error also emerges in the writings of a number of thinkers in the Continental tradition as a means of theorising life – and animal life in particular – at the margins of art, politics and ethics, and thus as a means of asking whether these peculiarly human endeavours are, in fact, constituted at the boundary between what we understand to be 'human' and 'animal'.

NOTES

1. Canguilhem, *The Normal and the Pathological*, p. 285.
2. Ibid., p. 126.
3. Ibid., p. 101.
4. See Bergson, *Creative Evolution*, Chapter 3.
5. Famously, Bertrand Russell on Bergson's 'revolt against reason' in his *History of Western Philosophy* (Woking: George Allen & Unwin, 1946), pp. 819–38.
6. Canguilhem, *The Normal and the Pathological*, pp. 128–9.
7. Michel Foucault, *The Birth of the Clinic* (London and New York: Routledge, 1989), p. 242.
8. Martin Jay, *Downcast Eyes: The Denigration of Vision in Twentieth-Century*

French Thought (Berkeley: University of California Press, 1993), p. 187.

9. See Elizabeth Haigh, *Xavier Bichat and the Medical Theory of the Eighteenth Century* (London: Wellcome Institute for the History of Medicine, 1984).

10. Nikolas Rose, 'Medicine, History and the Present', in *Reassessing Foucault: Power, Medicine and the Body* (London: Routledge, 1994), p. 49.

11. Elie During, 'A History of Problems: Bergson and the French Epistemological Tradition', in *The Journal of the British Society for Phenomenology*, 35:1, 2004, p. 7.

12. Michel Foucault, *The Archaeology of Knowledge* (London and New York: Routledge, 1989), p. 191.

13. Ibid., p. 72.

14. Ibid., p. 60.

15. Foucault, *The Birth of the Clinic*, pp. 4–5.

16. Ibid., p. 12.

17. Xavier Bichat, *Physiological Researches on Life and Death* (1800), in Daniel N. Robinson (ed.), *Significant Contributions to the History of Psychology 1750–1920* (Washington DC: University Publications of America, 1978), pp. 9–10.

18. Foucault, *The Birth of the Clinic*, pp. 174–5.

19. Ibid., p. 157.

20. Ibid., p. 188.

21. Bichat, *Physiological Researches*, p. 77.

22. Georges Canguilhem, 'Cell Theory', in *Knowledge of Life* (New York: Fordham University Press, 2008), p. 44.

23. See Foucault, *The Birth of the Clinic*, p. 210. Foucault argues, in the sole explicit reference to Bergson in *The Birth of the Clinic*, that Bichat had underlined in the field of medical research the superfluity of vitalist speculation: 'Bergson is strictly in error when he seeks in time and against space, in a silent grasp of the internal, in a mad ride towards immortality, the conditions with which it is possible to conceive of the living individuality. Bichat, a century earlier, gave a more severe lesson. The old Aristotelian law, which prohibited the application of scientific discourse to the individual, was lifted when, in language, death found the locus of its concept: space then opened up to the gaze the differentiated form of the individual.'

24. Bergson, 'Psycho-Physical Parallelism and Positive Metaphysics', in Gary Gutting (ed.), *Continental Philosophy of Science* (Oxford: Blackwell, 2005), p. 67.

25. Ibid., p. 65.

26. Ibid., p. 59.

27. Ibid., p. 62.

28. Ibid., p. 59.

29. Claude Bernard, *An Introduction to the Study of Experimental Medicine* (New York: Dover, 1957), p. 201.

30. Henri Bergson, 'The Philosophy of Claude Bernard' (1913), in *The*

Creative Mind: An Introduction to Metaphysics (New York: Citadel Press, 1992), p. 205.

31. See Canguilhem, *The Normal and the Pathological*, pp. 65–89.
32. Bernard, *An Introduction to the Study of Experimental Medicine*, p. 202.
33. Bergson, *The Creative Mind*, p. 204.
34. Claude Bernard, *An Introduction to the Study of Experimental Medicine*, p. 219.
35. Bergson, *The Creative Mind*, pp. 206–7.
36. Bergson, 'Psycho-Physical Parallelism and Positive Metaphysics', p. 61.
37. Ibid., pp. 62–3.
38. Henri Bergson, *Matter and Memory* (New York: Zone Books, 1991), p. 183.
39. Ibid., p. 13.
40. Ibid., p. 28.
41. Ibid., p. 31.
42. Ibid., p. 15.
43. Ibid., p. 180.
44. Bergson's opposition to idealism encompasses both its 'English' (attributed to J. S. Mill) and Kantian forms: 'My consciousness of matter is then no longer either subjective, as it is for English idealism, or relative, as it is for the Kantian idealism. It is not subjective, for it is in things rather than in me. It is not relative, because the relation between the "phenomenon" and the "thing" is not that of appearance to reality, but merely that of part to whole' (Bergson, *Matter and Memory*, p. 230).
45. Ibid., p. 181.
46. Ibid., p. 147.
47. Ibid., p. 148.
48. Bergson, 'Psycho-Physical Parallelism and Positive Metaphysics', p. 66.
49. F. C. T. Moore, *Bergson: Thinking Backwards* (Cambridge: Cambridge University Press, 1996), pp. 28–9.
50. Félix Ravaisson, *L'Art et les mystères grecs* (Paris: L'Herne, 1985).
51. Bergson, *Matter and Memory*, p. 102.
52. Ibid., p. 22.
53. Moore, *Bergson: Thinking Backwards*, p. 27.
54. Bergson, *Matter and Memory*, p. 10.
55. Ibid., p. 207.
56. Ibid., pp. 31–2.
57. Ibid., p. 21.
58. Bergson's circuit diagram expresses this simple, purely 'reflective' relation between subject and object: 'Our distinct perception is really comparable to a closed circle, in which the perception-image, going toward the mind, and the memory-image, launched into space, careen the one behind the other ... We maintain ... that reflective perception is a *circuit*, in which all the elements, including the perceived object itself, hold each other in a state of mutual tension as in an electric circuit, so that no disturbance

starting from the object can stop on its way and remain in the depths of the mind: it must always find its way back to the object from where it proceeds' (ibid., pp. 103–4).

59. Ibid., p. 58.
60. Ibid., p. 57.
61. P. A. Y. Gunter, 'Bergson and the War Against Nature', in John Mullarkey (ed.), *The New Bergson* (Manchester: Manchester University Press, 1999), pp. 168–82.
62. Ibid., p. 171.
63. Ibid., p. 175.

3. *Violence, Pathos and Animal Life in European Philosophy and Critical Animal Studies*

If it is our aim to come to a more effective way of confronting the issue of the treatment of non-human animals and, more specifically, the rearing and use of animals in scientific research, then a range of approaches from the European or 'Continental' tradition of philosophy (such as deconstruction or biopolitical analysis, for example) would seem to have the potential to overcome alternative and directly human-ist approaches to the question of the significance of animal life. The terms and designations according to which the lives of animals tend to be judged are inescapably humanist or anthropocentric (questions of rights, subjectivity and agency), while moral philosophy, in its dealings with moral agents and moral patients, is already defined in terms of certain human characteristics (rationality, symbolic use of language, etc.) to which non-human animals inevitably fail to conform. Therefore, we must conclude, other animals are simply not worthy of moral consideration.

One key move, which Jacques Derrida will come to embody, is to resist the tendency to frame discussions in terms of 'the animal' (partici-pating in a symbolic sacrifice that is supposedly constitutive of human identity), and instead to consider the fates of *animals*, or the actual bodies being subjected to the forces of regularisation, optimisation (via genetic engineering, etc.), and commodification in laboratory or intensively farmed conditions. An immediate difficulty is to constitute, convincingly, a form of resistance that matches up to or challenges the legislative 'readiness to hand' of the more traditional moral theories that carve up reality in terms of identifiable groups of 'insiders' and 'outsiders', or those to whom a law can apply and those to whom it cannot.

In this chapter, I will look at three ways of thinking the relations between animals and pathology that reflect some of the concerns of the field of critical animal studies, and some key responses in Continental philosophy that suggest moments of rupture or resistance within those debates, offering the potential for alternative conceptualisations of animal life. First of all, the use of animals for research into disease tends to be debated, principally within traditional moral philosophy, in terms of the possible justifications for violence against non-human animals. The problem at the heart of this use of what is essentially millions of individual animals in the UK alone (around 4.11 million 'procedures' performed in 2012 according to Home Office figures[1]) is that animals and humans are sufficiently homologous, biologically speaking, to yield useful experimental results, but not sufficiently alike for animals to merit moral consideration; typically, animal suffering tends to be outweighed by human benefits. In response, I will turn to Derrida's reflections on the meaning of *pathos* as suffering (or passive capacity), and how this reveals the limitations of ethical debates based on certain animal capacities and the concept of rights. I will then go on to examine the concept of animals as disease (or carriers of disease), and how this characterises Deleuze and Guattari's thinking of 'the Anomalous' as the disruptive feature of animal existence that persists across evolutionary, psychoanalytic and literary representations of the human/animal distinction. Finally, I will consider the implications of applying the mobile threshold of the normal and the pathological, which also implies the movement of the boundary between what is human and what is non-human, exemplified both in Foucault's analysis of the development of clinical medicine (as we saw in Chapter 2), and in his identification of pathological processes that escape or resist the exercise of biopower (or the techniques of power over life and death).

DERRIDA AND THE ETHICAL

Using Derrida's essay, 'The Animal That Therefore I am (More to Follow)', the problem I want to begin with concerns the use of the term 'the Animal' and its status as a general identifier. The word 'animal' is used to identify 'every living thing that is held not to be man'.[2] It is 'an appellation that men have instituted, a name they have given themselves the right and the authority to give to the living other'.[3] It also names that part of ourselves that we share with other animals, while helping to distinguish us from them: to be human is to be a rational animal, a political animal, the animal that has language, and so on.

   The essay begins with an encounter with a cat (one that catches him in the nude), an encounter that Derrida finds sufficiently surprising and perplexing to provoke questions in relation to a set of discourses in both traditional moral philosophy and in Continental or European philosophy, on the nature of the distinction between human and non-human animals, and the possibility of intersubjective relationships between them. Derrida attempts to set his analysis apart from this history, first in relation to other works – a long line of fictional cats in the history of literature – that he alludes to in the first part of the piece, by focusing on the specificity of this encounter with an animal, this one cat, in particular:

> When it responds in its name . . . it doesn't do so as the exemplar of a species called 'cat', even less so of an animal genus or kingdom. It is true that I identify it as a male or female cat. But even before that identification, it comes to me as *this* irreplaceable living being that one day enters my space, into this place where it can encounter me, see me, even see me naked.[4]

Derrida's essay is distinctive and *rare* in the area of Continental philosophy for its direct acknowledgment and engagement with the conditions in which animals, both those reared by humans and species living in the wild, are largely forced to live as a consequence of human intervention. Not all of these interventions are necessarily detrimental to animal life, but the main fact at hand is that what we understand about animals, and our attitudes towards them, have changed (or rather *intensified*) over the last two hundred years or so.[5] These changes have occurred in our conceptual understanding of organic life through developments in the life sciences (biology, zoology, genetics, etc.), but also in certain transformations of our relationship to animals through the activities of hunting and blood sports (from fox-hunting, bullfighting, rodeos, and even 'canned' hunting on the African continent), and present-day methods of farming and the 'exploitation of animal energy' (working animals).[6] It is a trajectory that has led to our present-day industrial-scale manipulation of animal life for the production of meat, leather and fur, entailing 'the reduction of the animal not only to production and overactive reproduction (hormones, genetic crossbreeding, cloning, etc.) of meat for consumption, but also of all sorts of other end products, and all of that in the service of a certain being and the putative human well-being of man'.[7]

This 'unprecedented' degree of subjection of the animal, Derrida writes, amounts to *violence*, and he goes on to compare this large-scale subjection of animal life to examples of genocide, and the death camps. Rather than simply making this comparison in order to elicit an emotional response, or to evoke *pathos*, Derrida draws attention to what has become the centre of moral philosophising about the status of animals, namely, the capacity to suffer, as originally put forward by Jeremy Bentham.

Bentham's re-statement of the question most pertinent to the problem of how we ought to treat other animals can be found in his *Introduction to the Principles of Morals and Legislation* (1824):

> The day *may* come when the rest of the animal creation may acquire those rights which never could have been witholden from them but by the hand of tyranny. The French have already discovered that the blackness of the skin is no reason why a human being should be abandoned without redress to the caprice of a tormentor. It may one day come to be recognised that the number of legs, the villosity of the skin, or the termination of the os sacrum, are reasons equally insufficient for abandoning a sensitive creature to the same fate. What else is it that should trace the insuperable line? Is it the faculty of reason, or perhaps the faculty of discourse: But a full grown horse or dog is beyond comparison a more rational, as well as a more conversable animal, than an infant of a day, or a week, or even a month, old. But suppose it were otherwise, what would it avail? The question is not, Can they reason? nor Can they talk? but, Can they suffer?[8]

This acknowledgment of a common capacity for suffering goes on to serve as the theoretical foundation for one of the most important contemporary proponents of a utilitarian approach to animal ethics, Peter Singer. For Singer, as argued in his 1975 book, *Animal Liberation*, the circle of moral consideration must be widened to include not just human beings but also non-human animals alike. The principle of equality upon which it is based is *not* a statement about an actual equality that exists between human beings and thus has no special application to human life alone.[9] If our treatment of other humans is *not* guided by an *actual* equality between us (differences of race, sex, intelligence, etc., are all overridden by the principle of equality in moral terms), then we must, in our moral judgements, appeal to some other criterion. For Singer, this would be the equal consideration of interests, and those interests would be defined primarily in terms of Bentham's identification of our common capacity to suffer. Consequently, as Singer points out in *Animal Liberation*, actions undertaken in favour of the interests of our own species alone beg comparison with other forms of imposed inequality:

> The racist violates the principle of equality by giving greater weight to the interests of his own race when there is a clash between their interests and the interests of another race. The sexist violates the principle of equality by favouring the interests of his own sex. Similarly the speciesist allows the interests of his own species to override the greater interests of other species. The pattern is identical in each case.[10]

Singer's most significant counterpart/interlocutor in late twentieth-century moral debates on animal equality, Tom Regan, argues in his 1988 *The Case for Animal Rights* (in part against Singer's utilitarian position) that progress towards serious consideration of animal rights will come from the categorisation of animal lives as 'subjects of a life' (so possessing beliefs and desires; perception, memory, and a sense of the future, including their own future, for example). For Regan those who satisfy the subject-of-a-life criteria have a distinctive kind of inherent value and are not to be viewed or treated as mere receptacles.[11] Thus perfectionist theories that value individuals based on their possession of certain virtues (e.g. intellectual skills) must be rejected 'because it would justify the unjust exploitation of the less virtuous (e.g. the less intelligent) by the more virtuous'.[12] Utilitarianism, based on the equal consideration of interests (or pleasures) is rejected because of its failure 'to account for the full range of the wrongful acts that may be done to moral agents . . . or because . . . [it fails] to account for the full range of our direct duties to moral patients (a central defect of rule utilitarianism)'.[13] Adopting a utilitarian position, for example, would not necessarily be incompatible with the continuation of some experimentation on animals, and some killing of animals for food, if it could be outweighed by an overall improvement in the condition of animal life and well-being.

THE FACE OF THE OTHER

The search for categories adequate to the differences between humans and our 'others', including other animals, while also allowing us to establish ethical relations with others, defines Emmanuel Levinas' writings on alterity, in which we begin to see some instances of rupture and resistance in our thinking of the foundations of intersubjective relations.

In an essay entitled 'Is Ontology Fundamental?', Levinas finds in the encounter with another human being a kind of relation which does not involve the subordination of a particular being under a universal concept: 'I have neglected the universal being that he incarnates in order to remain with the particular being he is.'[14] The *encounter*, for Levinas, is a passive relation to the other which is not the same as *knowledge* of the other (if knowledge involves a hierarchy of universal over particular), and is not therefore an ontological relation. That is, the intersubjective relation (between one human subject and another) now formulated as the *encounter* is an *ethical* one since 'the encounter with the other consists in the fact that despite the extent of my domination and his slavery, I do not possess him'.[15] In Levinas' thought it is, finally, the *face* that provokes this ethical relation, signifying a being's 'infinite resistance to our power'.[16]

Levinas' success in presenting a truly passive, non-violent account of intersubjectivity is questioned by a number of commentators, including Matthew Calarco and, ultimately, Derrida, as I will explain shortly. The most significant problem arises in regard to the face, and who or what counts as having a face. In 'The Name of a Dog, or Natural Rights'[17] Levinas recounts a story from his time in an internment camp in which a dog comes to visit the prisoners, and whose affectionate attachment to them formed over a number of days, as Levinas writes, shows that the dog was able to recognise the humanity of the prisoners even in a context which had otherwise dispossessed them of their humanity. However, Levinas goes on to admit in an interview ('The Paradox of Morality') that it is still problematic to attribute a face to other animals:[18] 'I cannot say at what moment you have the right to be called "face". The human face is completely different and only afterwards do we discover the face of an animal. I don't know if a snake has a face. I can't answer that question.'[19]

In his book, *Zoographies*, Matthew Calarco provides one of the most sustained recent engagements, from a Continental perspective, with the questions of animal identity and the human/animal distinction. Using the works of Heidegger, Levinas, Agamben and Derrida, Calarco exposes the remnants of anthropocentric prejudices in philosophical texts which purport to confront the domination of the human over the animal. Calarco's book is characterised by its exploration of the alternative sense of 'ethics' provided by Continental thinkers in the post-Husserlian phenomenological tradition such as Levinas and Derrida who focus on radical politics and concepts of 'the Other'. Calarco's response to Levinas is, however, qualified by the claim that Levinas' definition of the ethical relation can be read in a way that renders it far less anthropocentric than his account of the ethical encounter at first allows.

> The question of who the Other is, that is, of who might make a claim on me and thus be morally considerable, cannot be determined with any finality. Unless we proceed from this kind of generous agnosticism, not only are we bound to make mistakes . . . but we also set up the conditions of possibility for the worst kinds of abuses toward those beings who are left outside the scope of moral concern.[20]

Levinas' own hesitation in ascribing a face to other animals is, according to Calarco, a hesitation to follow through the consequences of his own philosophical position. 'If we are to learn anything from Levinas', Calarco explains, 'it is that ethical experience occurs precisely where phenomenology is interrupted and that ethical experience is traumatic and not easily captured by thought.'[21] It is the faces of those creatures that are most radically 'Other' for us that surely bring about this rupture in our thinking that is the occasion for the ethical response.[22]

Derrida's response to a certain thread in the history of Western philosophy, including the thought of Levinas, turns the focus back on to comparisons between human and non-human life in terms of the primacy of rationality. According to Derrida, Levinas simply follows a line of other thinkers from Aristotle and Descartes, and up to Heidegger, by reinforcing the existence of a gulf between humans and animals, on the basis of a certain capacity: the capacity to reason and to talk (i.e. with status in relation to *logos*). While Levinas' position, as I have just discussed, seems to be fairly malleable (Calarco's criticism of Levinas amounts to a kind of defence of his philosophy in so far as thinking the Other can work in relation to animal life), the heritage of defining the status of animals against the measure of human life still clearly lies behind Levinas' work. Heidegger, for his part, is notable for his categorisation of the animal as 'poor in world' compared to the world-forming human being, though not as impoverished as the 'world-less' stone.[23] In another typical example of wordplay, Derrida accentuates this problematic tendency to take the measure of non-human animal life by comparing it with a set of characteristics that are identified as specifically human (and therefore of superior value), for example, those animals that we can teach to converse with us in our own language are deemed to be the most intelligent (apes, pigs, dogs). What is significant, for Derrida, about Bentham's identification of the importance of the capacity to suffer, does not simply concern the question of our commonality with other animals (as discussed by Singer, Regan, et al.) that might make us improve our treatment of them. Rather, it is the primacy accorded to one's active *capacities*, such as the capacity to reason and to speak (*logos*). By contrast, the question, 'Can they suffer?' refers to a certain *passivity*, a 'not-being-able-to' (playing on the French word, *pouvoir*):

> what counts at the origin of such a question is not only the idea of what transitivity or activity (being able to speak, to reason, etc.) refers to; what counts is rather what impels it toward this self-contradiction . . . 'Can they suffer?' amounts to asking 'Can they *not be able*?' And what of this inability [*impouvoir*]? What of the vulnerability felt on the basis of this inability? What is this nonpower at the heart of power?[24]

This is, essentially for Derrida, a question of the common *mortality* of all living beings (shared experiences of compassion, nonpower and vulnerability), marking the importance of the concept of *pathos* in our understanding of organic and, in particular, animal life. In the final section of this chapter, I will discuss further aspects of the meaning of 'pathos', as set out by Foucault, but for now I want to turn next to the contribution that Gilles Deleuze makes to our understanding of animals in resistance to certain limited zoological categorisations of animal life, and how this response forms the basis for an alternative ethical relation between human and non-human animals.

BECOMING-ANIMAL

In their discussion of, amongst other examples, bird song, Deleuze and Guattari in *A Thousand Plateaus* focus on the respects in which such phenomena in animals are connected with the institution of territories. A territory, for our purposes, is a space within which specific meanings and functions (and all other kinds of structure) can be enclosed. The critique in this section of *A Thousand Plateaus* is directed at zoologists who make aggression the main trait in animals for the institution of a territory. Deleuze and Guattari's argument is that there are all sorts of other animal behaviours that are acts of 'territorialisation', such as song, display, and what is essentially the use of 'tools' in order to construct a territorial display (e.g. birds that use pieces of wood, stone, leaves and fruits to build a display) as well as the various forms of social interaction amongst animal groups. And so, ask Deleuze and Guattari:

> Can this becoming, this emergence, be called Art? That would make the territory a result of art. The artist: the first person to set out a boundary stone, or to make a mark ... The expressive is primary in relation to the possessive; expressive qualities, or matters of expression, are necessarily appropriative and constitute a having more profound than being.[25]

A number of key features of 'becoming-other' are set out by Deleuze and Guattari, commencing with the general idea of 'becoming' as the basis for reality instead of 'Being', and according to which processes of coming into existence do not occur through resemblance but rather through the formation of 'unnatural alliances'. Also key is the concept of the multiplicity (molecular, imperceptible) of packs which opposes the integrity (molar, unified) of the family (or socially permitted and socially regulated relationships). Becomings, they explain, come about through a relation with The Anomalous (or The Other reconfigured):

> there is a sinister choice since there is a 'favorite' in the pack with which a kind of contract of alliance, a hideous pact, is made; there is the institution of an assemblage, a war machine or criminal machine, which can reach the point of self-destruction; there is a circulation of impersonal affects, an alternate current that disrupts signifying projects as well as subjective feelings, and constitutes a nonhuman sexuality; and there is an irresistible deterritorialization that forestalls attempts at professional, conjugal, or Oedipal reterritorialization.[26]

Finally, there is a process of 'deterritorialisation' (for our purposes, the freeing up of meaning, accepted usage or function) which resists being reincorporated into familiar and familial structures or relationships (for example, the Oedipus complex is the familial structure that most char-acterises interpretations of the human condition in the modern age).

By commencing with a discussion of the terms with which naturalists categorise organic (and animal) life, Deleuze and Guattari invite us to think not just about the problematic reduction of organic systems to relations of 'kinship, descent, and filiation', but also the possibilities inherent in later evolutionary theory for thinking about the nature of 'Relation' across different disciplines. That is, the natural historical approach was restricted to categorisations in terms of resemblance (between A and B as discrete quantities) only, whereas later evolution-ism would start to think in terms of production (from A to x), that is, in terms of a *qualitative* change from one species to another.[27] Thinking 'relation' from the point of view of natural history can thus be said to occur along the following lines: series and structure. In the case of thinking in terms of series, 'I say *a* resembles *b*, *b* resembles *c*, etc.; all of these terms conform in varying degrees to a single, eminent term, perfection, or quality as the principle behind the series. This is exactly what the theologians used to call an analogy of proportion.'[28] On the other hand, in a relation of structure: 'I say *a* is to *b* as *c* is to *d*; and each of these relationships realises after its fashion the perfection under consideration: gills are to breathing under water as lungs are to breath-ing air; or the heart is to gills as the absence of a heart is to tracheas [in insects]. This is an analogy of proportionality.'[29] Such a procedure characterises the science of homologies, the founding figure of which was Geoffroy Saint-Hilaire. The tendency to refer any living thing back to its origin in a perfect idea or model recalls the tradition of think-ing nature in terms of a Great Chain of Being (as we saw in Chapter 1 above). Deleuze and Guattari reinforce this point in attributing the tendency to view nature along these lines to the residues of theological conceptions of Nature as 'an enormous *mimesis*'; here, we could refer back to a Platonic realm of Forms in relation to which all creatures exist as greater or lesser imitations.[30]

Now, Deleuze and Guattari's effort to think about an alternative relation proceeds in terms of what they call 'blocks of becoming' that are not reducible to relations of terms in a series or structure, and that do not result in a 'third term' that is a synthesis of the previous two (this would be a conventional relationship of generation or heredity).[31] For example, in the case of the thynnine wasp (*Chiloglottis trapeziformis*) and the 'sexually deceptive' orchid flower (*Neozeleboria cryptoides*) that relies upon it for pollination, a relationship has evolved between these two distinct species that does not result in a 'wasp-orchid' hybrid.[32] One could remark that all relationships between flowers and their pollinators describe this kind of unproductive 'coupling', but the wasp/orchid example starkly proves the point in the elaborate mechanisms adopted by the flower 'in order to' ensure pollination occurs: the flower has evolved a shape that mimics the appearance, and in some instances the pheromones, of female wasps such that male wasps are sufficiently duped and attracted to the flower to attempt to mate with it. Unlike other pollinators (birds and insects that feed on nectar), the wasp gets no 'reward' for its response, but rather ends up by carrying the pollen of the flower to other orchids, thus serving only the orchid's needs. Other examples of these unproductive relationships (lacking in a synthesis of a third term) include a genetic relation between baboons (but no other primates) and domestic cats 'effected by a C-virus'.[33] We might also think about the composition of our cells which, it is argued, may well be 'inhabited' by primitive micro-organisms (mitochondria are the energy-converting components of our cells, and these are not synthesised by our bodies, but are instead only ever passed on from mother to child). This movement between terms (which is not one towards homogeneity) is called 'involution' which is 'to form a block that runs its own line "between" the terms in play and beneath assignable relations'.[34] This neo-evolutionism studies animals 'by populations that vary from milieu to milieu or within the same milieu; movement occurs not only, or not primarily, by filiative productions but also by transversal communications between heterogeneous populations'.[35]

The next element of the attempt to think through this alternative type of relation is the importance of the animal as, fundamentally, a multiplicity. This is where we return to examples in art (literature) as well as the processes just discussed of contagion, symbioses or cross-species relationships that do not yield new syntheses (wasp-orchid, cat-baboon, as well as epidemics). In response to some potential misreadings of the significance of animals in this text, Deleuze and Guattari distinguish three kinds of animal. Again, this is a kind of taxonomy of the animals that appear in art and literature, and which have invited interpretation predominantly along the first two lines, but which may also carry the potential to be read alternatively in terms of becoming-animal, as Deleuze and Guattari present it. First of all, Oedipal animals count among them the very type of 'individuated animals' that Derrida claims we overlook (and we will see in Chapter 6 how Haraway responds to these categorisations by both Derrida and Deleuze). Such animals are merely sentimental, Oedipal animals each with its own petty history, 'my' cat, 'my' dog. These animals invite us to regress, draw us into a narcissistic contemplation, and they are the only kind of animal psychoanalysis understands, the better to discover a daddy, a mommy, a little brother behind them (when psychoanalysis talks about animals, animals learn to laugh): *anyone who likes cats or dogs is a fool.*[36]

The second category describes 'animals with characteristics or attributes; genus, classification, or State animals; animals as they are treated in the great divine myths',[37] while a third category, clearly the favoured alternative for Deleuze and Guattari, describes 'demonic animals':

> pack or affect animals that form a multiplicity, a becoming, a population, a tale ... Or once again, cannot any animal be treated in all three ways? ... Schools, bands, herds, populations are not inferior social forms; they are affects and powers, involutions that grip every animal in a becoming just as powerful as that of the human being with the animal.[38]

The 'risk' of identification with one of the first two animals is essentially the risk of reductionism: artistic expression that is occasioned by some sort of image of an animal can always be interpreted (psychoanalytically) as a symbol of the artist's familial relationships, or as the affirmation of one's status within a wider social hierarchy. 'Demonic' animals point to something else altogether: entering into a creative relation with the world that causes traditional meanings to slide, to defer, or to disintegrate. Part of Deleuze and Guattari's analysis is thus concerned with seeking out examples of such animal becomings in art, in order to illustrate the respects in which various artworks resist traditional interpretation along lines that reinforce the original integrity of subjectivity. Thus their discussion of 'The Anomalous' looks at a number of examples of such demonic animals, primarily in literature (e.g. Moby Dick). Here, it is interesting to note the etymology of the word 'anomaly':

> It has been noted that the origin of the word *anomal* ('anomalous'), an adjective that has fallen into disuse in French, is very different from that of *anormal* ('abnormal'): *a-normal*, a Latin adjective lacking a noun in French, refers to that which is outside rules or goes against the rules, whereas *anomalie*, a Greek noun that has lost its adjective, designates the unequal, the coarse, the rough, the cutting edge of deterritorialization. The abnormal can be defined only in terms of characteristics, specific or generic; but the anomalous is a position or set of positions in relation to a multiplicity.[39]

The artist or philosopher who enters into an 'anomalous' relationship through the artwork is effecting a form of thought that operates outside of traditional psycho-social boundaries. All of the 'apparatus' of the State, the family, the career, the obedience to law, are there to reinforce the integrity of the Subject (including the control and reinforcement of subjective identity through the reduction of 'deviant' modes of thought to recognisable, if pathological, familial structures), and to avoid the 'spilling over' of *abnormal* behaviours into common life. The 'unnatural participations' of becomings-other explore what is outside these boundaries, and force the proliferation of meaning, purpose or utility.

This overflow of meaning and purpose is the effecting of a *deterritorialisation*, or a *line of flight*.[40] Recall that human art was identified with 'art' in animals (bird song, other forms of display) which was linked to the institution of a territory. In the processes of becoming-animal described above, human art (creative activity) does not only reinforce territorial boundaries (Subject, Family, State), it can also deterritorialise: it can effect the disintegration of meaning. Of course, this does not mean that new territories (meanings) do not immediately take the place of old ones, but this attests to the processes of deterritorialisation and reterritorialisation that thinkers and artists must constantly undergo in their works.

Deleuze and Guattari appeal to a number of thinkers in the course of this work, including Nietzsche, Bergson, Leibniz and also Spinoza. In Spinoza's thought, which Deleuze and Guattari point to for its peculiar account of substance (taken as a *critique* of Substance), one approach that is of particular significance for thinking through this alternative perspective on relations between terms is the use of 'Affect' as the basis for ethics. Affects take primacy above adherence to The Good, or concepts of virtue or nobility (i.e. that to which traditional moral philosophy appeals in determining how one ought to act in a given situation). Individuals or *bodies*, from a Spinozist point of view, must be understood in terms of their power to act: 'To the relations composing, decomposing, or modifying an individual there correspond intensities that affect it, augmenting or diminishing its power to act; these intensities come from external parts or from the individual's own parts.'[41] That is, one's conduct can be guided or determined by the extent to which any given situation increases or decreases one's power to act. There are good encounters and bad encounters. Thus, instead of analysing a body in terms of organs and functions, the task is to understand and enumerate its affects. It is in this sense, Deleuze continues, that a Spinozist ethics is an ethology.[42]

To illustrate the ethological approach to the study of animal bodies, Deleuze and Guattari make reference to the work of Jakob Von Uexküll, whose theory of the *Umwelt* took affects as the basic unit of experience in the worlds of non-human animals:

the Tick, attracted by the light, hoists itself up to the tip of a branch; it is sensitive to the smell of mammals, and lets itself fall when one passes beneath the branch; it digs into its skin, at the least hairy place it can find. Just three affects; the rest of the time the tick sleeps, sometimes for years on end, indifferent to all that goes on in the immense forest. Its degree of power is indeed bounded by two limits: the optimal limit of the feast after which it dies, and the pessimal limit of the fast as it waits.[43]

The essential point here is that an ethological approach does not attempt to explain the tick's behaviour in terms of the functions of different parts of its body, but rather in terms of the whole set of relations into which the body of the tick enters, and how such relations effect increases or decreases of the body's power to act.[44]

There are many contentious issues in Deleuze's texts, and just one of them is the implication that this fusing of ethics and ethology has for a range of problems in traditional moral philosophy. Recall the traditional ethical relations based on either the capacity to suffer (Bentham, Singer) or the intrinsic value of life (all life, from complex mammals to trees and whole ecosystems, as argued by Regan and also Paul Taylor). Just as the example of the tick gives us an affect-based understanding of the relationships between different animals that is ethical in the precise sense of an *ethology*, the examples of becoming-animal that Deleuze and Guattari refer to (in art, literature and case studies in psychoanalysis) are presented as examples in which human thinkers establish ethical (ethological) relationships with non-human animals. According to Deleuze and Guattari, such becomings are rife in aspects of human existence that tend to be marginalised and interpreted as symbols of some pathological grasp of real situations (in relation to familial structures, personal identity and adherence to law):

> When Hofmannsthal contemplates the death throes of a rat, it is in him that the animal 'bares his teeth at monstrous fate.' *This is not a feeling of pity*, as he makes clear; still less an identification. It is a composition of speeds and affects involving entirely different individuals, a symbiosis; it makes the rat become a thought, a feverish thought in the man, at the same time as the man becomes a rat gnashing its teeth in its death throes. The rat and the man are in no way the same thing, but Being expresses them both in a single meaning in a language that is no longer that of words, in a matter that is no longer that of forms, in an affectability that is no longer that of subjects. *Unnatural participation.*[45]

A Deleuzian (Spinozist) ethic cannot treat of subjects who appeal to some higher order of The Good, but must look instead at the variety of ways in which we relate to others without reducing that relation to one of hierarchy, identity or normality.

Rosi Braidotti (in her 2008 book, *Metamorphoses*) contends that this is a valuable contribution to the animal question, in its attempted critique of the hierarchies in which animal life tends to be subordinated. For Deleuze, it is not that we are trying to establish the criteria for inclusion of animals into the human circle of moral consideration. We are, instead, exploring the ways in which we relate to non-human animals at the level of affects. It is, of course, deeply contentious whether Deleuze's formulation is satisfactory, but it is certainly an attempt to make explicit the implications of an ontology based on difference for a politics that has historically been based on identity.[46] Braidotti goes on to argue that Deleuze does *not* romanticise the way in which human beings can interact with other animals. However, does the idea of becoming-animal really operate with anything more than the abstract figure of 'The Animal'? If, as Braidotti claims, this is Deleuze's response to Heidegger, then it remains questionable whether it is sufficiently successful in bridging the gulf between the world-forming human and the impoverished animal.[47] Indeed, as I will go on to argue in Chapter 6 in relation to the work of Donna Haraway, it is Derrida's call for an acknowledgement of our treatment of individual animals that more convincingly overcomes the risk of romanticising human/animal interactions. We are severely limited in our capacity to think animality if, as Deleuze and Guattari do, we idealise or create a hierarchy of animal types with which we can form privileged bonds. Rather, the most significant interactions that we have with other animals really only occur in those moments when we are confronted with our responsibility for – or *power* over – the lives of particular animals, of whatever species, whether at the levels of health and economic policies (regarding wild, urban or farmed animals), or in our everyday interactions (regarding pets, and 'working animals').

THE POWER OVER LIFE AND DEATH

In the third of his volumes of the *History of Sexuality*, entitled *The Care of the Self*, Michel Foucault presents an analysis of the practice of medicine in Ancient Rome, and notes that the practices of philosophy and medicine are intertwined:

> They do in fact draw on a shared set of notions, whose central element is the concept of 'pathos'. It applies to passion as well as physical illness, to the distress of the body and to the involuntary movement of the soul; and in both cases alike, it refers to a state of passivity, which for the body takes the form of a disorder that upsets the balance of the humors or its qualities and which for the soul takes the form of a movement capable of carrying it away in spite of itself.[48]

If we turn to Foucault's concept of biopower, we can see how it reinforces that what it means to be human *and* animal is a shared capacity for suffering: *pathos* as the body's vulnerability. If part of this vulnerability is *susceptibility to disease*, in what respects is this significant in the consideration of non-human animals today in relation to problems associated with increasing human populations? For example, we need only look at the growth of bio-medical research, some of which might be in response to an increasing and ageing population with an associated increase in the prevalence of conditions such as cancer and dementia, the need to combat epidemics and pandemics of various kinds, and the increasing medicalisation of previously 'normal' or invisible conditions; and then the categorisation of a number of animal species as 'pests' (e.g. rats, mice, pigeons, foxes), which compete with us for space and resources, particularly in urban areas. Could it not be said that what dominates discourse about animals is the boundary between the normal and the pathological? What, then, are the consequences for our thinking of the human/animal divide in relation to the conditions in which millions of animals are kept by humans today: in laboratories, in intensive or factory farms, in circuses or zoos, including also animals such as horses and dogs bred for racing, and the whole array of other domestically reared animals kept as pets and 'working animals' (guide dogs, police dogs, etc.)?

In Foucault's descriptions of biopower and biopolitics I want to draw particular attention to the linkages with his references to medicine and health (that attest to shifts in the divide between life and death, which becomes a divide between normal and pathological). In the *History of Sexuality*, Foucault summarises various historical shifts in the exercise of sovereign power, ranging from the sovereign's right (using the Roman patriarch as an example) to dispose of the lives of his children and his slaves, to the definition of a diminished sovereign power with the right to kill only when its existence is in jeopardy. And, Foucault continues, 'this formidable power of death . . . now presents itself as the counterpart of a power that exerts a positive influence on life, that endeavours to administer, optimise, and multiply it, subjecting it to precise controls and comprehensive regulations'.[49] This power over life presents itself in two basic forms: first in the form of disciplines or an 'anatomo-politics of the human body' where the body is seen as a machine, and power over it focuses on 'its disciplining, the optimisation of its capabilities, the extortion of its forces, the parallel increase of its usefulness and its docility, its integration into systems of efficient and economic controls'.[50] Second, in power as regulatory control, forming a biopolitics of the population, focused on 'the species body, the body

imbued with the mechanics of life and serving as the basis of the biological processes: propagation, births and mortality, the level of health,
life expectancy and longevity, with all the conditions that can cause
these to vary'.[51]

This is essentially the development of public health as a policy area
for the State to regulate, and of the measurement of population health
as a means of ensuring the integrity (the normal functioning) of the
State, while regulations communicated to and implemented among the
population (e.g. via health screening, recommended dietary intakes,
etc.) treat the population 'as [an] object towards which mechanisms are
directed and [as a new collective] *subject* that is called upon to conduct
itself in certain ways'.[52]

In what respects, then, does the normal/pathological division dominate our discourse about animal life? As Foucault notes, even with the
exercise of biopower – of discipline and regulatory control over life
itself – there are still always forces that escape its governance, such as
the risks of drought and crop failure leading to famine and the spread
of disease.[53] Another important aspect is 'the action of *the norm*, at
the expense of the juridical system of the law'.[54] That is, the operation of law becomes organised around a set of norms: 'A normalising
society is the historical outcome of a technology of power centred on
life.'[55] In other words, what is sought, at the end of these organising
processes, is an ideal or optimal condition of life. Richard Twine argues
that thinking in terms of biopower helps to dissolve the distinction
between human and animal life, since the exercise of power over life
itself does not necessarily reinforce species boundaries.[56] Consequently,
the aim for this 'optimal condition of life' should apply to all species,
including those raised for food and the production of pharmaceuticals.
But I would argue that what we find in Foucault's analysis of this
'optimal life' is also the tendency to ascribe a 'pathological status' to
certain forms of life, the use of this category to reinforce the hierarchy
of human over animal, and the associated justifications for violence
against non-human animals in order to protect and promote human
health. Foucault himself has described his analyses as attempts to 'see
how [scientific, political and ethical] processes may have interfered with
one another in the formation of a scientific domain, a political structure, a moral practice'.[57]

Here one might use the example of recent UK public health policy and
related initiatives in the area of 'healthy eating'. As part of this there has
been an increased emphasis on and scrutiny of farming practices (e.g.
the pathological conditions of intensively reared animals passing into
the food chain – anything from BSE or Foot and Mouth disease to the

high fat content of meat from animals kept in conditions that prevent exercise and other 'normal' behaviours). The *moral* issues surrounding the treatment of animals under intensive farming conditions and in laboratories for scientific research are, at the same time, influenced by the *scientific or medical* issues of how to maximise the health of the human population, and the economic consequences of certain farming practices for a country's 'economic health'. Following Foucault, we can see here a demonstration of the cross-cutting of forces: scientific, medical, economic, political issues influencing and, it could be argued, dominating ethical debates on the value of animal life.

One final example might be the moves made towards the normalisation of previously pathological conditions, such as the milder forms of Autistic Spectrum Disorder. Temple Grandin, who writes about her own experience of being autistic, most notably in *Thinking in Pictures* (1995) and *Animals in Translation* (2005), discusses the resonances between autistic traits and certain tendencies and patterns of animal behaviour.[58] My reference to Grandin is not intended to romanticise autism; there is no suggestion of a superior kind of perception, though some parallels can be drawn with a Bergsonian account of intuition as an enlarged perception that precedes the formation of rigid conceptual or logical boundaries. The study of autistic traits, as Grandin presents it, offers insights into normal animal sensory processing; but this is not to say that severe autism equates to the normal functioning of 'lower' animals. Rather, such studies show, for example, that hypersensitivity in autistic individuals can range from debilitating to mildly socially inconvenient, while in regard to other animals they can lead to a greater understanding of forms of consciousness in which sense-based information is primary and dominant, as distinct from language-based thought. The prioritisation of speech may well be normal for most humans, but the delays or obstacles to its development or normal functioning reveal that sensory domination need not be intellectually crippling for people with (or without) a diagnosis.

Returning, in conclusion, to Derrida's critique of Western philosophical logocentrism, Grandin's analysis suggests that human thought is not necessarily always (or fundamentally) language-based. As Grandin herself suggests, understanding of autism is increasing our understanding of just how wide the array of human functioning is. The underdevelopment of language-based skills and thought processes in certain individuals is not simply the identification of a pathological condition, but carries with it a reconsideration of what constitutes 'normality', gained through a reconsideration of the nature of animal life and our own fundamentally animal condition.

NOTES

1. Home Office, *Statistics of Scientific Procedures on Living Animals, Great Britain* 2012 (London: The Stationery Office, 2013). Available at <https://www.gov.uk/government/publications/statistics-of-scientific-procedures-on-living-animals-great-britain-2012> (last accessed 8 December 2013).
2. Jacques Derrida, *The Animal That Therefore I Am* (New York: Fordham University Press, 2008), p. 31.
3. Ibid., p. 23.
4. Ibid., p. 9.
5. Ibid., p. 25.
6. Ibid.
7. Ibid.
8. Jeremy Bentham, *An Introduction to the Principles of Morals and Legislation* (Oxford: Clarendon Press, 1823), Chapter 17, sn. 4, n., p. 235.
9. Peter Singer, *Animal Liberation*, 2nd edn (London: Pimlico, 1995), p. 5.
10. Ibid., p. 9.
11. Tom Regan, *The Case for Animal Rights* (London: Routledge, 1988), p. 243.
12. Ibid., p. 263.
13. Ibid., pp. 262–3.
14. Emmanuel Levinas, 'Is Ontology Fundamental?', in Adrian T. Peperzak, Simon Critchley, and Robert Bernasconi (eds), *Basic Philosophical Writings* (Bloomington and Indianapolis: Indiana University Press, 1996), p. 7.
15. Ibid., p. 9.
16. Ibid., p. 10.
17. Emmanuel Levinas, *Difficult Freedom: Essays on Judaism* (Baltimore: Johns Hopkins University Press, 1990), pp. 151–3.
18. See Emmanuel Levinas, 'The Name of a Dog, or Natural Rights' and 'Interview', in Peter Atterton and Matthew Calarco (eds), *Animal Philosophy: Essential Readings in Continental Thought*, (London: Continuum, 2004), pp. 49–50; for the full interview, see Emmanuel Levinas, 'The Paradox of Morality', in Robert Bernasconi and David Wood (eds), *The Provocation of Levinas: Rethinking the Other* (London: Routledge, 1988), pp. 168–80.
19. Levinas, 'Interview', in Atterton and Calarco (eds), *Animal Philosophy*, p. 49.
20. Matthew Calarco, *Zoographies* (New York: Columbia University Press, 2008), p. 72.
21. Ibid., p. 73.
22. Derrida sets out elsewhere, for example in an interview called 'Eating Well', the bias in the history of Western thought to what he calls *carnophallogocentrism*. See *Points: Interviews, 1974–1994* (Stanford: Stanford University Press, 1995), pp. 255–87.

23. Martin Heidegger, *The Fundamental Concepts of Metaphysics* (Bloomington: Indiana University Press, 1995), pp. 186–200.
24. Derrida, *The Animal That Therefore I Am*, pp. 27–8.
25. Gilles Deleuze and Félix Guattari, *A Thousand Plateaus* (London: Athlone, 1982), pp. 315–16
26. Ibid., p. 233.
27. Ibid., p. 234.
28. Ibid.
29. Ibid.
30. Ibid., pp. 234–5.
31. See Brett Buchanan, *Onto-ethologies*, Chapter 4 (New York: SUNY Press, 2008).
32. F. P. Schiestl et al., 'The Chemistry of Sexual Deception in an Orchid-Wasp Pollination System', *Science*, 302, 17 October 2003, p. 437.
33. R. E. Benveniste et al., 'Detection of Baboon Type C Viral Sequences in Various Primate Tissues by Molecular Hybridization', *Journal of Virology*, 14:1, 1974, p. 56: 'The partial homology between type-C-related information in the DNA of domestic cats and various Old World monkeys suggests the possibility of horizontal transmission between the progenitors of these animals at some point in evolution.'
34. Deleuze and Guattari, *A Thousand Plateaus*, p. 238.
35. Ibid., p. 239.
36. Ibid., p. 240.
37. Ibid.
38. Ibid., p. 241.
39. Ibid., pp. 243–4.
40. Ibid., p. 249.
41. Ibid., p. 256.
42. Deleuze is certainly not unique in writing about animals from the point of view of ethology. Mary Midgley adopts an ethological approach to her study in *Beast and Man* (London and New York: Routledge, 1979) of the diverse ways in which human life can be productively compared with animal life and behaviour.
43. Deleuze and Guattari, *A Thousand Plateaus*, p. 256.
44. Ibid., pp. 256–7.
45. Ibid., p. 258.
46. On the question of a feminist philosophy and politics, we are again asked to consider the alternatives to thinking in terms of the 'binary machine' (i.e. attempting to tip the balance in favour of the inferior term in the binaries: man/woman, human/animal, white/black, etc.). Thinking in such terms is to remain at the level of a 'molar politics', an identity politics that presupposes fully formed subjects and established social and political structures of State, law and family: 'It is, of course, indispensable for women to conduct a molar politics, with a view to winning back their own organism, their own history, their own subjectivity: "we as women . . ." makes

its appearance as a subject of enunciation. But it is dangerous to confine oneself to such a subject, which does not function without drying up a spring or stopping a flow . . . It is as deplorable to miniaturise, internalise the binary machine as it is to exacerbate it; it does not extricate us from it. It is thus necessary to conceive of a molecular women's politics that slips into molar confrontations, and passes under or through them. When Virginia Woolf was questioned about a specifically women's writing, she was appalled at the idea of writing "as a woman." Rather, writing should produce a becoming-woman as atoms of womanhood capable of crossing and impregnating an entire social field, and of contaminating men, of sweeping them up in that becoming' (ibid., p. 276).

47. Rosi Braidotti, *Metamorphoses* (Oxford: Blackwell, 2002), pp. 137–8.

48. Michel Foucault, *The History of Sexuality, Volume 3: The Care of the Self* (London: Penguin, 1990), p. 54. Cf. also p. 136: 'The medical regimen proposes, then, a sort of animalisation of the *epithumia*; that is, a subordination, as strict as possible, of the soul's desire to the body's needs.' This is because animal desire is not affected by representations of the desired thing; it is simply a need. And p. 142: Roman medicine 'uncovered, at the root of sexual acts, an element of passivity that was also a source of illness, according to the double meaning of the word *pathos*. The sexual act is not an evil; it manifests a permanent focus of possible ills.'

49. Michel Foucault, *The History of Sexuality, Volume 1: An Introduction* (New York: Vintage Books, 1990), p. 137.

50. Ibid., p. 139.

51. Ibid.

52. Michel Foucault, *Security, Territory, Population: Lectures at the Collège de France, 1977–1978* (London: Palgrave Macmillan, 2009), p. 43.

53. Foucault, *The History of Sexuality, Volume 1*, p. 143.

54. Ibid., p. 144.

55. Ibid.

56. Richard Twine, *Animals as Biotechnology: Ethics, Sustainability and Critical Animal Studies* (London: Earthscan, 2010).

57. Michel Foucault, 'Polemics, Politics, and Problemizations: An Interview with Michel Foucault', in Paul Rabinow (ed.), *The Foucault Reader* (Harmondsworth: Penguin, 1984), p. 386.

58. Temple Grandin, *Thinking in Pictures* (London: Bloomsbury, [1995] 2006); Temple Grandin and Catherine Johnson, *Animals in Translation* (London: Bloomsbury, 2006).

4. From Animal-Machines to Cybernetic Organisms . . .

Despite the life-centred view of organic activity that is found in the work of Henri Bergson, it was acknowledged, not least by Bergson himself, that the formulation of a positive concept of life was extremely problematic, requiring a reversal of the normal direction of utility-driven thought. As we saw in Chapter 2, Canguilhem and Foucault, in their analyses of the development of physiology and medicine, showed how the classification of species and life itself underwent rapid reconfiguration in terms of a new understanding or incorporation of error, disease and death into life. We then saw how this shift engendered a different attitude towards animal life, and the senses in which animality could serve as an opening onto or element of resistance in thought and life, such as biopolitical resistance. The key characteristic of life that offers itself up for study becomes less impetus or drive, and more deviation, anomaly and morbidity. But what about an even more extreme shift in understanding life in terms of 'non-life': life born of non-living processes, the possibilities of thinking life in terms of not simply mechanism, but rather information and crystallisation? What happens to our ability to relate to living organisms if we can reduce them to information systems (is this simply a modern equivalent of a Cartesian concept of animal automata)?

To approach these questions, this chapter will focus in further detail on the claims of Georges Canguilhem, introduced in Chapter 2, that productive (as opposed to reductive or derogatory) insights into organic processes have been gained through an engagement with 'non-life': death, disease and monstrosity. I will ask to what extent this perspective from non-life informs or transforms our understanding of animal life, and what kind of role remains for 'positive' concepts of life in the face of the predominance of pathological and exceptional modes of being in the development of philosophical and biological accounts of living processes. I will also examine the movement from thinking animality as mechanistic in nature (animal-machines) to a transformed view of mechanism in the phenomenon of the cybernetic organism, where the natural and the technological are newly fused and provoke a new thinking of the concept of the organic. Through the thought of Canguilhem, Whitehead and Haraway, over the next three chapters I will look at this development of the concept of the organic and its complex trajectory towards a greater sense of the affinities between the organic and the technological but also, at the same time, a growing appreciation of the complex systems that constitute or engender life, its consequent specificity or uniqueness, as well as the relations that living things continue to propagate, all of which are integral to a shared animal existence.

THE MEANING OF NON-LIFE

In Canguilhem's analyses and advocacy of the study of concepts of 'non-life', these include not only ideas such as monstrosity and pathology, but also, as I will go on to discuss, the specific example of the 'carrier of heredity' used by Darwin to underpin his theory of evolution by natural selection. This idea is just one of many examples of what Canguilhem refers to as *scientific ideologies*. Such ideas, although not empirically demonstrable in themselves, have historically served as the foundations for a number of scientific theories. We have seen how Canguilhem is best known for his writings on the subject of normal and pathological life, and how pathological phenomena have become the most reliable means by which we can study what we would otherwise call the normal or healthy states of a living thing. In the context of the history of science, Canguilhem advocates the focus on pathological phenomena as the modern phase of development in biological and medical thinking that has ranged from the mechanism of Descartes and the teleological description of life in Kant to the rejection in the nineteenth century of vitalism as a theoretical basis or grounding assumption for the life sciences. Recall, for example, that both Canguilhem, in *The Normal and the Pathological*, and Foucault, in *Madness and Civilisation* and *The Birth of the Clinic*, have written about the conjunction of previously disparate sciences – anatomy, physiology, psychology, chemistry and physics. All of these sciences proved instrumental in the formation of new attitudes towards the relation between life and death, new vocabularies for understanding and ultimately curing diseases, and the introduction of new legislative frameworks for stemming the flow of disease in the population through public health directives.[1] Another example of this movement towards 'mortal' concepts of life would be the development of the Freudian theory of the death instinct, in which life was definable as the slowing-down of the process of degradation of energy. This was itself a theory that benefited from the conjunction of biological and psychological sciences with Carnot's principles of thermodynamics, though not until sometime after Claude Bernard's development of an experimental physiology.[2]

Until the end of the eighteenth century, however, the Aristotelian method of studying living things facilitated the study of life, without actually having to articulate exactly what that life was in itself: 'Life forms were classified according to similarities and differences in their parts (or organs), actions, functions and modes of life.'[3] As we saw earlier, efforts to understand evolutionary change were centred on the end-products of these processes (the resulting or surviving organisms) rather than the force that carried them to that point, but it seemed that two alternative (but by no means mutually exclusive) routes could be taken in the development of the life sciences. The first would be to reinstitute a theory of vital force or impetus, and this would emerge, for example, in the line of French Spiritualist philosophers culminating in the theory of the *élan vital* in Bergson's *Creative Evolution* at the turn of the twentieth century. The second would be to continue physiological research not with an assumption of a vital principle, but with an analogical model specific to the processes or functions being studied. In an essay on 'Experimentation in Animal Biology', Canguilhem discusses the benefits and limitations of analogical reasoning (in the absence of a direct concept of life) in order to discover the functions of individual organs. Alluding also to the issue of the use of live animals for research, Canguilhem illustrates the use of analogy in a passage from an eighteenth-century medical thesis (Deisch, 1735) on the study of the effects of the removal of a dog's spleen:

> It is not surprising that the insatiable passion for knowledge, armed with its blade, has penetrated the secrets of nature and has applied a licit violence to dogs, cheaply procured victims of natural philosophy – a violence that could not be applied to man without crime – in order to ascertain the exact function of the spleen by examining lesions resulting from the ablation of this viscus and thus whether such and such an author's proposed explanation is true and certain . . . [O]ne hopes to observe . . . in dogs surviving an ablation of the spleen some phenomenon that would have been impossible to observe in dogs with the spleen intact.[4]

While acknowledging that this passage is 'loaded' (for its admission of violence towards non-human animals), Canguilhem's focus here is on the way in which it summarises a number of important characteristics of biological experimentation.[5] In particular, animal vivisection is a *substitute* for direct access to knowledge: for example, the removal of the spleen from the animal is designed to discern the function of the organ by observing the effects on the whole animal once the organ has been removed; and experiments are carried out in order to verify a theory. In the longer extract from the thesis, comparison is made between this experimental method and the practice of neutering (namely, castration) in farmed animals, as a means of controlling both breeding cycles and general behaviour. This, Canguilhem observes, indicates the way in which analogy plays an important role in instituting experiments (if neutering an animal changes its behaviour, then we can gain useful knowledge from observing what happens when other organs are removed). It also indicates that there is a link between (a) animal experiments for the purposes of verification and (b) other 'biological techniques' used, for example, in the rearing or breeding of animals. The first manifestation of 'non-life' is, then, a reduction of the animal body to a tool for the acquisition of knowledge, and as a malleable object that can serve as a substitute for life.

The concept of scientific ideology that Canguilhem propounds in *Ideology and Rationality in the History of the Life Sciences* (1977) aims for the preservation of the balance between, on the one hand, theories in science that overstep the bounds of scientific rigour and verification, and, on the other hand, theories that employ tools such as analogy or substitution (for example, in the use of animal bodies) in order to provide as complete a picture of a system's functions as possible in the absence of direct evidence. Now, although my focus here is not on the general merits of identifying scientific ideologies in the history of science, it is worth recounting what Canguilhem understands by the term 'ideology', as his narrative in the specific case of Darwinian evolution is also, in effect, a defence of the use of analogy in place of direct knowledge or evidence of a particular living process, despite the risk it carries of overstepping the bounds of verifiability. In Darwin's case, an analogy served in place of the vehicle of heredity or what, today, we understand to be DNA, since at the time of the publication of *The Origin of Species* (1859) such a vehicle had not yet been adequately conceived for the purposes of supporting the theory of natural selection.

The influence of Gaston Bachelard[6] on Canguilhem has been well noted, as has his acknowledged debt to Michel Foucault, which Canguilhem writes about in the introduction to *Ideology and Rationality in the History of the Life Sciences*, stating, in a fit of modesty, that his own analyses of the life sciences have not exposed their conditions of possibility as rigorously as Foucault's studies have done. Nevertheless, what Canguilhem does provide us with are four ways of thinking the meaning of ideology. Firstly, 'the ideologies of scientists' include the example of the concepts of 'nature' and 'experience' used by eighteenth-century scientists that were essentially philosophical terms used to place science in a wider cultural context. The three remaining ways of understanding ideology are outlined as follows:

> a. Scientific ideologies are explanatory systems that stray beyond their own borrowed norms of scientificity.
> b. In every domain scientific ideology precedes the institution of science. Similarly, every ideology is preceded by a science in an adjunct domain that falls obliquely within the ideology's field of view.
> c. Scientific ideology is not to be confused with false science, magic or religion. Like them, it derives its impetus from an unconscious need for direct access to the totality of being, but it is a belief that *squints* at an already instituted science whose prestige it recognises and whose style it seeks to imitate.[7]

For Canguilhem, the important point to note is the way in which his usage of the term differs from the familiar Marxist usage according to which an ideology's main function is to prevent human beings from understanding their true relation to reality: 'Ideology exists, according to Marx, wherever attention is diverted from its proper object.'[8] The term 'ideology', as Canguilhem uses it, returns to an even earlier usage borrowed from eighteenth-century French philosophy. Destutt de Tracy, in his 'Memoire sur la faculte de penser', as Emmet Kennedy outlines,[9] intended that the term, meaning 'the science of ideas' in Greek, would provide an alternative account to those based on metaphysical ideas (or forms) or psychological ideas, both of which implied that it was somehow possible to uncover the true function or form of the soul or mind.[10] Rather, an ideological analysis would simply be concerned with the relations between ideas and how they develop or fall out of use. Condillac (as well as Locke), for example, whose work Tracy saw as part of the 'Ideological School', is today seen as a very early predecessor of Wittgenstein in the primacy he accords to language or 'signs' in the formation of thought (as opposed to some soul or animating principle shaping the way we think and act). This is not to say, however, that Ideology was originally 'neutral'. On the contrary, Tracy's intention was for it to form the basis for all of the other human sciences (grammar, logic, education and morality) and ultimately the regulation of society itself.[11] In the lineage from Cabanis and Tracy to the work of Maine de Biran (which would engender the nineteenth-century French Spiritualist movement, the latter moments of which we have seen in the philosophy of Bergson), Biran's study of certain 'ideological phenomena' (unconscious intellectual habits, the association of ideas, etc., previously identified by Tracy) underlined that:

> Ideology was supposed to study intellectual habits, not succumb to them like schoolmen, Platonists, Scotists, Thomists, and Cartesians, who only prove [as Tracy had stated] 'that we accept from the same pen both what is proven and what is only apparently so, that the authority of the man is still considerable and that the force of demonstration does not prevail alone.'[12]

Kennedy also notes how 'Ideology' came to be used pejoratively, culminating perhaps in the positivism of Auguste Comte who would attempt to pare philosophy back to the study of facts, criticising the Ideologues along the way for concentrating too heavily on Ideas rather than such facts.

Canguilhem, then, takes the term 'ideology' in its original meaning as 'the science of the genesis of ideas', where ideas are treated 'as natural phenomena determined by the relation between man, a living, sensitive organism, and his natural environment'.[13] Bearing this meaning in mind, we can think evolutionism as a scientific ideology that has separated into modern evolutionary theory (with Darwinism as an integral part of its history) on the one hand, and, on the other, 'evolutionist ideology' such as is to be found in Herbert Spencer's application of evolutionary theory outside of its own domain and into the social domain, thus rendering it an ideology in the Marxist sense.[14] One of the key conditions of possibility for the development of modern evolutionary theory was a shift in the relations between the sciences; for example, the greater integration of a number of the life sciences, which previously defined themselves in terms of disparate methodologies, as well as a new recognition of the significance of physical and chemical laws and properties in biological objects, leading to the development of modern biochemistry. Canguilhem gives examples of the state of the life sciences in the nineteenth century, which initially provided little in the way of theoretical foundations for evolution by natural selection. Amongst them the science of physiology was seen by its theorists as an a priori, laboratory-based science, looking at individual cases and establishing functional constants rather than fluctuations. It also looked at regulatory mechanisms that helped an organism to achieve relative autonomy from its environment.[15] In other words, physiology was ill-equipped to furnish Darwin with a model for understanding how an organism can, or indeed must, adapt internally to changes in its external environment. Cell theory, against the grain of the other sciences, aligned more easily with Darwin in so far as the science of embryology, for example, 'incorporated the new dimension that [Darwin] was attempting to introduce into the science of biology, namely, time . . . The fossil was petrified time; the embryo, operative time; the rudimentary organ, retarded time.'[16] Finally, in the case of microbiology, Louis Pasteur helped to establish against the theory of spontaneous generation that life only comes from life, but this idea that 'like produces like' would again weaken the force of any idea of transmutation.[17] The importance that Canguilhem identifies in the work of Pasteur, however, is the move that it initiates away from the study of micro-organisms simply as 'agents of organic decay and infection'.[18] As Canguilhem notes:

> Pasteur did not find the solution to the pathological problems of living things in the realm of the living. He found it by shifting his attention to crystals, to those geometric embodiments of pure mineral substance. He did not find it by treating living things as though they were inert . . . but by distinguishing living things from inert substances in terms of their most general structural properties.[19]

Finally, Canguilhem goes on to recount the role of the work of Gregor Mendel, whose insights gained through experiments with heredity in the sweet pea were passed over in his own time but rediscovered in the twentieth century, leading up to the discovery of the structure of DNA. This later conjunction of the work of Crick, Watson and Darwin (via Mendel) also exemplifies the way in which the history of science is to be read as a series of ruptures and innovations. That is, 'progress came when biology created for itself a "new scientific object" . . . a "polyscientific" or "interscientific" object, by which [is meant] not an object treated by more than one discipline but one constructed as the explicit result of collaboration among several disciplines.'[20] In these terms DNA 'exists not as an artifact but as a "superreal", nonnatural object'.[21] And, because of the gap in knowledge in Darwin's own time, Canguilhem continues, 'we know that Darwin was right to have posed the problem of evolution in terms that he was obliged to invent'.[22] In summary, the conjunction of disparate sciences has now given rise to a 'new biology' which is 'the science of an object . . . obtained by a series of renunciations of traits previously held to be characteristic of living things, such as sexual reproduction and enzymatic reactions. Life is now studied as far as possible as though it were nonlife, as devoid as possible of its traditional attributes.'[23]

This second meaning of non-life, as 'superreal, non-natural object', when analysed retrospectively, reveals itself to be the common, though as yet unformulated, principle behind modern evolutionary theory. In the use of analogues of life (the laboratory animal, the superreal object) it is also possible to trace developments beyond the mechanistic concept of the animal, though this is not an unproblematic shift or progression from mechanism to vitalism (or organicism), nor conversely from a mysterious concept of soul or vitality to physical reductionism. Rather, there is a complex interplay of a problematised mechanism with respect to animal bodies, and a refinement in our understanding of the processes of life in concert with the development of ever more complex information-processing systems.

TECHNICS

In the following sections I will examine a number of links between the thought of Georges Canguilhem and that of Donna Haraway, with particular focus on their analyses of the changing boundaries between the mechanical and the organic, or the physical and the vital, culminating in an acknowledgement of the impact of modern informatics on accounts of all levels of life from the structure of DNA to the structures of society. While the previous section tracked a development in experimental physiology underpinned by the reduction of animal bodies to tools that can be manipulated to reproduce a range of physiological effects at the convenience of the researcher, in the following I will outline Canguilhem's problematisation of the dualism between mechanism and organism. This reconfigures Bergson's insights into the continuity between utility-driven perception and human science and technology, though with a less pronounced division between natural technique and human technology. I will then go on to consider the trend in Haraway's writings on cybernetic organisms towards the alignment of organic processes with information systems, and how this offers a view of science and technology as forces for both the reduction of the living to 'code', but also for the critique of models of human and animal agency.

In his essay, 'Machine and Organism', Canguilhem confronts the problem of the attempts in the history of the sciences to explain organic bodies in terms of machines, and why its inverse, the explanation of machines in terms of organisms, has not emerged as the dominant model of explanation. Indeed, Canguilhem will go on to extol the hierarchy of organism over machine in order to raise questions about the relation between technology and science, and thereby return us to a questioning of the place of teleological or finalistic thinking in the study of living processes.

The dominance that mechanistic models have attained in the explanation of organic phenomena obscures the fact that definitions of machines already presuppose the existence of a 'mechanic', of human artifice, behind the mechanism. It is to this hidden presupposition that Canguilhem will appeal in order to argue that the organism remains the ultimate explanatory principle for mechanical action and the development of human life as the development of *technique*. At the root of the problem of mechanical explanation is a simple confusion of the definition of the *machine* as an 'artificial construct, a work of Man, whose essential function depends on mechanisms', reliant upon a mechanism or an 'assemblage of deformable parts, with periodic restoration of the relations between them',[24] and the definition of a *motor force* that is responsible for generating movement. Canguilhem notes from examples of early human technology, such as the use of animals to drive machines, that such machines often relied upon some form of external force. It is the capacity of machines to store energy long after the human or animal effort has ceased that contributes to the forgetting of the dependency of mechanisms on the action of living beings. This forgotten relationship immediately brings to mind Descartes' ascription of the status of automata to soul-deprived animals, and Canguilhem notes that such a reduction of animal life to mechanical action 'can only be conceived once human ingenuity has constructed apparatuses that imitate organic movements: for example, the launching of a projectile, the back-and-forth movement of a saw – apparatuses whose action (their construction and activation aside) takes place independently of man'.[25]

Descartes' separation of human and animal both draws upon a theoretical presupposition of the priority of rationality or the capacity to judge over the capacity to suffer (animals do not judge, therefore they do not have souls), and presupposes that machines can exist independently of some motor force: thus animals can exist as mere automata. For Canguilhem, Descartes' position on animal life is immediately comparable to Aristotle's view on slavery: it is devalorised in order to justify its often violent exploitation as an instrument for the use of human beings.[26] Thus, Canguilhem observes the interdependence of the 'theoretical mechanisation of life and the technical utilisation of the animal'.[27] The denial of natural purposes, so elegantly mitigated in Kant's espousal of the regulative use of teleological models in his *Critique of Judgement*, allows for the promotion of human interests above the rest of nature, because only human subjects can be considered as ends in themselves.

As we saw in Chapter 1, Bergson's turn to an 'external finality' entails a rejection of a theory of internal finality (teleology in the senses described by both Leibniz and Kant) for its reliance on a pre-given concept of the whole of the organism that is artificially divisible into identifiable parts, each with its own 'cause'. Internal finality is also rejected for its basis within a model of time that serves merely as the medium within which the product (the evolved organism) is unfolded according to its pre-established specifications. Similarly, the mechanistic explanation is to be rejected for its basis in an ineffective time, and for the assumption that physico-chemical analyses of organic elements are sufficient to yield knowledge of the functions of an organism, and of the products of evolutionary processes. Canguilhem's response to this problem returns us to Descartes, specifically his *Treatise of Man*, demonstrating that the theory of animal-machines it contains merely provides a description of certain mechanisms that ultimately refer back to a builder-God. This God has 'set the direction once and for all; the direction of the movement is included by the builder in the mechanical device that executes it'.[28] The opposition between mechanism and finalism is erroneous, and the relation between the two is no more than a tautology since mechanisms must necessarily refer back to some form of human purpose: 'A machine is made by man and for man, with a view toward certain ends to be obtained, in the form of effects to be produced.'[29]

What, then, is there to be gained from a reversal of the hierarchy of machine over organism? As we have seen, for Canguilhem, we thereby gain knowledge of the correct order of explanation of mechanical operations. In order to properly understand what a particular 'mechanism' does, it is necessary first to observe it in its functioning state, whereas observations of the form and structure of its parts alone do not reveal enough about its purpose or use.[30] In distinction to Kant's teleological explanation, Canguilhem (like Bergson) concludes that such analysis reveals the specificity of biology and biological explanation. Not only is it *useful* to think of organic phenomena in terms of natural purposes, it is also futile to derive biological organisation from mechanical models. If machines are distinguishable by their narrowness of function, living organisms possess a distinctive *plasticity* of function, such as the adaptability of organs to different functions if the original organ is damaged or destroyed, as in the case of childhood aphasia cited by Canguilhem: 'Hemiplegia on the right side is almost never accompanied by aphasia, because other regions of the brain ensure the language function. And when aphasia appears in a child under nine years old, it dissipates rapidly.'[31]

Canguilhem's affirmation of a fundamental relation of interdependency between an organism and its environment is inherited from Kurt Goldstein, the early twentieth-century neurophysiologist, whose key work, *The Organism*, was published in 1934. In response to observations made on brain-damaged soldiers, Goldstein propounds the idea that an environment determines an organism's 'direction', but, at the same time, the organism helps to shape its milieu. Here, Goldstein refers to cases in neuro-pathology to illustrate the way in which a sick organism will tend towards attempting to re-order its environment in order to accommodate its new pathological way of functioning. For example, individuals with damage to certain parts of the brain were observed taking particular care to order and align objects in a room; we can also point to the example of 'stereotyped' behaviour in captive animals; in each case controlling one's environment means controlling one's set of sensory stimuli.[32]

> Recovery is a newly achieved state of ordered functioning, that is, responsiveness, hinging on a specifically formed relation between preserved and impaired performances. This new relation operates in the direction of a new individual norm, of new constancy and adequacy (contents). Every recovery with residual defect entails some loss in 'essential nature'. There is no real substitution.[33]

Furthermore, as Goldstein goes on to claim, in a phrase echoed by Canguilhem, the discovery of biological knowledge is akin to the capacity of the organism to become adequate to its environmental conditions.[34]

These observations on the nature of interaction between organism and environment, and the behavioural adaptations arising from them, have notably influenced Maurice Merleau-Ponty, particularly in his *Phenomenology of Perception*, in which traditional philosophical dualisms between mind and body, and between body and world, are problematised in the light of Goldstein's experimental observations. Merleau-Ponty discusses the specificity of biological functioning in his account of the phenomenon of phantom-limb sensation, and its explanation in the operation of the bodily schema:

> When the insect, in the performance of an instinctive act, substitutes a sound leg for one cut off, it is not . . . that a stand-by device, set up in advance, is automatically put into operation and substituted for the circuit which is out of action. But neither is it the case that the creature is aware of an aim to be achieved, using its limbs as various means, for in that case the substitution ought to occur every time the act is prevented, and we know that it does not occur if the leg is merely tied . . . [T]he insect projects the norms of its environment and itself lays down the terms of its vital problem.[35]

Resisting explanation here in purely mechanical or intellectual terms, Merleau-Ponty shares Canguilhem's aim of drawing out the distinctive features of organic functioning and the complex set of relations that biological entities form with their environments and with one another. This act of substitution of one organ by another, to cope with damage or environmental changes, brings us back to Canguilhem's discussion of the history of technology, specifically those accounts in which tools can be interpreted as extensions of human organs. A further development of this interpretation of the continuity of technology and nature is also to be found in Richard Dawkins' extension of his theory of the selfish gene to incorporate a theory of 'the extended phenotype' or the extension of genotypic identity to phenotypic expression not just in the immediate physical characteristics of the organism in question, but also in the cases of 'tool use' by non-human animals:

> an animal artefact, like any other phenotypic product whose variation is influenced by a gene, can be regarded as a phenotypic tool by which that gene could potentially lever itself into the next generation. A gene may so lever itself by adorning the tail of a male bird of paradise with a sexually attractive blue feather, or by causing a male bower bird to paint his bower with pigment crushed in his bill out of blue berries. The details may be different in the two cases but the effect, from the gene's point of view, is the same.[36]

In these terms we can say that it is not that *Homo sapiens* is separable from the rest of organic life with the advent of technology (the application of knowledge as simply a selection or distortion of the real), but rather that technology as the extension of already biological apparatuses attests to the continuity of human life with nature.[37]

THE CYBORG

The suggested continuity between technology and biological 'technique' is developed in Donna Haraway's recognition of the need to think human and animal life in terms of 'hybridity', emerging not simply in the light of late twentieth-century technological developments, as if a more powerful metaphor for the organism was furnished by the 'information age', but perhaps more in tune with the implications of Canguilhem's reversal of the machine-organism hierarchy. Thinking human life in continuity with nature, as Bergson, followed by Canguilhem, argued, means that characteristics that were historically held to be distinctively human (even consciousness itself, following Bergson's line of argument as discussed in Chapter 1) are found in diffused or divergent forms across the living spectrum. We are no longer able to classify in terms of traditional taxonomies, but rather, as we saw in the writings of Deleuze and Guattari, we must begin to think relation in altogether different, that is, proliferated terms (humans in complex relation to other animals and the technologies we use to perform everyday tasks).

While the focus of Haraway's 'Cyborg Manifesto' (1991), which was originally conceived in the mid-1980s with reference to the Reagan administration's grand defence project named 'Star Wars', is the inter-action of socialist-feminism, technology and writing, I want to place particular emphasis on the concepts of relation, organic life and the 'informatics of domination' that are set out in the essay.

The image of the cyborg serves as a model for thinking about what we might call the taxonomical breakdowns that present themselves in our attempts to think the concept of life together with (or in opposition to) modern technologies. As I have outlined in the first three chapters of this study, the human/animal boundary is breached from a number of directions: evolutionary theory (from Bergson to Gould) and physiology attest to problematisations of concepts that have hitherto reinforced our distinctiveness from other animals (from species identity, to the apparent *telos* of human evolutionary paths), while the exception-based modelling of physiological analysis and pathological anatomy presents us with patterns of disease integral to living bodies (as opposed to attacking from without) that reinforces both the interdependency of micro-organic and macro-organic life and the commonality of human and animal life-towards-death. Furthermore, as Haraway points out, when we examine features such as 'language tool use, social behaviour, mental events, nothing really convincingly settles the separation of human and animal'.[38] Thus, whether new technologies have equipped us to scrutinise life at a microscopic level to discover ever decreasing units of difference between humans and animals, or, as in the case of tool use, to demonstrate that technique is less specific to human culture than pre-viously assumed, the fusion of the machine and organism in the figure of the cyborg describes this 'disturbingly and pleasurably tight coupling'.[39]

The second boundary is that of the organism and the machine. Whereas Canguilhem argued that the organic ultimately served as model and motive force behind mechanical devices, Haraway notes that modern machines effect the boundary shift in a way that primi-tive machines were unable to, the latter being merely a mockery of human life. Examples of the modern variety might include the graft-ing of machines to organic bodies (from monitoring devices such as electrocardiographs and electroencephalographs to life-enhancing pacemakers), or the exploitation of viruses and stem cells to construct new bonds between 'natural' bodies and artificial body parts, all manipulations that take place at the level of code. In *How We Became Posthuman*, Katherine Hayles outlines how many of us could now be thought of as cyborgs in the technical sense:

> including people with electronic pacemakers, artificial joints, drug-implant systems, implanted corneal lenses, and artificial skin. A much higher percentage participates in occupations that make them into metaphoric

cyborgs, including the computer keyboarder joined in a cybernetic circuit with the computer screen, the neurosurgeon guided by fiber-optic micros-copy during an operation, and the adolescent game player in the local video-game arcade.[40]

Add to this the aforementioned electroencephalographs and electro-cardiographs, and we witness the cybernetic fusions of organism and instrument at all levels of human life: including, ultimately, the moni-toring of individual bodies, yielding information on flows of productiv-ity and disease within and between populations (as Foucault noted in the development of centrally governed systems of public health). Furthermore, the cyborg model of modern warfare is equally applicable to today's increasingly non-human face of warfare (as it was to Reagan's Star Wars project to which Haraway refers) exemplified by the drone: 'coded by C3I, command-control-communication-intelligence'.[41]

At a higher level of generality, perhaps, is the boundary between the physical and the non-physical that modern machines straddle: 'Our best machines are made of sunshine; they are all light and clean because they are nothing but signals, electromagnetic waves, a section of a spectrum, and these machines are eminently portable, mobile. People are nowhere near so fluid, being both material and opaque. Cyborgs are ether, quintessence.'[42]

While some of the above boundary transgressions might seem, at first sight, to be largely beneficial in their rethinking of human and animal life in terms of 'naturecultures' (no longer separable into nature *or* culture, as Haraway will go on to underline in her *Companion Species Manifesto*), the critical force of the cyborg image lies in its internal duality, split across the utility it possesses for both the exercise of power or 'the final imposition of a grid of control on the planet' on the one hand, and the possibilities for resistance and critique on the other, in 'lived social and bodily realities in which people are not afraid of their joint kinship with animals and machines, not afraid of permanently partial identities and contradictory standpoints'.[43]

INFORMATION AS DOMINATION

Haraway's analysis of the 'informatics of domination' plays out the duality of the cyborg in two series of descriptive terms: for example, Nature/Culture, sex, labour, Mind in one series, and their counterpart descriptors, such as fields of difference, genetic engineering, robotics and Artificial Intelligence in the other. The new code-based terms of the latter series demonstrate the need to think power-relations no longer even in the biopolitical terms so potently set out by Foucault, as the exercise of power over life and death. Braidotti emphasises here Haraway's subtle indebtedness to Foucault, but argues that

> while sharing a great deal of Foucault's premises about the modern regime of truth as 'bio-power', Haraway also questions his redefinition of power. Haraway notes that contemporary power does not work by normalised heterogeneity any more, but rather by networking, communication redesigns and multiple interconnections. She concludes that Foucault 'names a form of power at its moment of implosion'.[44]

Haraway provides an example of this new communications or code-based strategy in the categorisation of women's capacities to give birth, but this can be extended to the whole range of modern public health measures, commencing with epidemiological analysis of morbidity rates, the identification and comparison of disease prevalence amongst different populations (e.g. increased rates of diabetes and heart disease in certain groups), and the formulation of preventative and curative strategies to address those morbidities (from cancer screening to vaccination and immunisation programmes). Such processes are witness to the dispersal and reformation of human subjectivities as rates and tendencies of not just productivity, but reproduction, disease and mortality:

> No objects, spaces, or bodies are sacred in themselves; any component can be interfaced with any other if the proper standard, the proper code, can be constructed for processing signals in a common language. Exchange in this world transcends the universal translation effected by capitalist markets that Marx analysed so well.[45]

Whereas Foucault notes threats to the exercise of biopower such as crop failure and outbreaks of disease, at the level of description that Haraway offers, the key threat becomes that of the *interruption of communication*, the outcome of stresses upon the systems in question. This threat to the grid of control thus opens up the space for the productive fragmentation or forms of resistance that constitute the complementary aspect of the cyborg image. Adopting a critical stance towards the retrospective classification of feminist movements, which has served to force (or enforce) affinities between otherwise divergent groups, Haraway seeks to avoid the 'totalising dream' of a common female language or code.[46]

Haraway's ambitions for an alternative feminist discourse that is more inclusive of disparate voices echoes Julia Kristeva's openness to Freudian psychoanalysis (despite its male-centred theories of the mechanisms of repression, as Simone de Beauvoir pointed out in *The Second Sex*), offering a more subtle reading of Freud's theory of the castration complex in order to move beyond both Freud himself and the characterisation of his thought as a denigration of women. First, the fear of castration manifests itself in 'imaginary formations' in the neuroses of both sexes and, as Kristeva goes on to note, it is not the apparently sexist terms of the theory that are the most significant, but rather the unconscious operation itself that is merely indicated by the theoretical framework that Freud happened to adopt. Kristeva is then able to accentuate two key aspects of Freud's thought. The first is that the castration fantasy is hypothesised to be the origin or foundation or ground of what 'unceasingly functions in neurotic discourse'.[47] It is simply posited as a 'best-fit' scientific theory which allows us to explain a whole series of phenomena arising in neurotic discourse. Kristeva likens this to the 'big bang' theory in physics, which we do not see direct evidence of, but a range of phenomena (such as background radiation, or signs of an apparently expanding universe) can be explained with reference to this origin until a better theory is proposed. Echoing, then, Canguilhem's analysis of the importance of ideologies and analogies in scientific discourse, Kristeva argues that Freud's castration fantasy merely serves as a ground or unifying theory used to interpret neurotic discourse. The second key aspect (in the later Freud, followed by Lacan) is that the emphasis need not be on the fear of castration taken by itself, but rather on the expression of something that is indeed fundamental for all of us: the acquisition of language based on 'separation from a presumed state of nature, of pleasure fused with nature so that the introduction of an articulated network of differences, which refers to objects henceforth and only in this way separated from a subject, may constitute *meaning*'.[48] Fear of castration, or the castration complex, operates as the 'major referent' in the operation of separation. What is significant is that it is lack or desire that constitutes the subject's insertion into language, and 'it would be just to emphasise its extension to all that is privation of fulfilment and of totality; exclusion of a pleasing, natural and sound state: in short, the break indispensable to the advent of the symbolic'.[49]

Women, Kristeva notes, have often complained about being left out of the 'socio-symbolic contract'; language has not afforded them the ability to articulate the full range of experiences of women, including the relation to their own bodies: 'A therefore difficult, if not impossible, identification with the sacrificial logic of separation and syntactical sequence at the foundation of language and the social code leads to the rejection of the symbolic – lived as the rejection of the paternal function and ultimately generating psychoses.'[50] And this rejection of the symbolic, an escape from the logic of castration as the basis for the start of language, can be exemplified in two types of counter-investment in, or withdrawal from, the symbolic: first, the grasping and subversion of the symbolic, usually in extremist or deadly terms (such as participation in 'terrorist' movements); second, the exploration of the individual's relation with this contract and the exploration, by women, of the shattering of language through art and literature: 'to find a specific discourse closer to the body and emotions, to the unnameable repressed by the social contract'.[51]

For Donna Haraway, alternatives to such linguistic totalisation are sought in forms of writing that struggle against language or perfect communication and instead explore the 'illegitimate fusions of animal and machine' that 'make Man and Woman so problematic, subverting the structure of desire, the force imagined to generate language and gender, and so subverting the structure and modes of reproduction of "Western" identity, of nature and culture, of mirror and eye, slave and master, body and mind'.[52]

FROM ORGANISM TO CODE

Recall that Canguilhem, in his analysis of Darwinian evolution's rise to scientific 'orthodoxy', pointed to a 'dematerialisation' of matter in physics and chemistry and a concomitant 'devitalisation' of life in biology – all of which is linked to developments in technology, for example microscopy, and allows for the 'making strange' of familiar objects. These shifts can also be summarised by way of a number of observations by Haraway, in 'The Biopolitics of Postmodern Bodies: Constitutions of Self in Immune System Discourse' (1988), in which she focuses on the modern science of immunology as an example of the way in which accounts of self and body have shifted from 'organism' to 'code', though this is by no means an unproblematic interpretation, as the example of immunology demonstrates.

The basic idea of a body's immune system, its system of defence against disease – and disease denotes, first of all, attack by foreign bodies (bacteria, viruses, etc.) – presupposes that there must be a form of self-recognition by the organism/body for it to recognise what is foreign to it: 'That is, the immune system is a plan for meaningful action to construct and maintain the boundaries for what may count as self and other in the crucial realms of the normal and the pathological.'[53] Haraway goes on to map changes in the science of immunology in terms of the changes in the definition of an organism. The key transition, for our purposes, is from (a) the body understood as a centrally organised and hierarchical division of labour to (b) the body as coded text (as exemplified by the aims of the Human Genome Project). And under this latter definition 'disease is a subspecies of information malfunction or communications pathology; disease is a process of mis-recognition or transgression of the boundaries of a strategic assemblage called self'.[54]

Yet, Haraway continues, the immune system analysed in terms of its genetic structure displays high rates of mutation in the processes used to create its arsenal of surface receptors and antibodies, and thus 'makes a mockery of the notion of a constant genome even within "one" body ... The immune system is everywhere and nowhere. Its specificities are indefinite if not infinite, and they arise randomly; yet these extraordi-nary variations are the critical means of maintaining individual bodily coherence.'[55] The displacement of questions of the 'source' of life or the 'final cause' of a living organism in favour of questions about the conditions under which an organism functions optimally (the science of physiology) is (returning to Canguilhem) achieved through a devi-talisation of life, or a renewed conception of living processes from the perspective of non-living phenomena, such as the process of crystallisa-tion. Here, one can immediately compare this to Haraway's analysis not only of the shift that occurs from the hierarchically organised body to living bodies as coded texts, but also of the problematisation of the self-identity and readability of the body. The very relation between the organism and its environment, rather than affirming the boundaries of the organism, is one in which it constantly seeks to accommodate or acclimatise itself to its surroundings, which, as Haraway's example of immunity demonstrates, suggests an organic identity that is fundamen-tally fractured. It is in the very definition of an organism to exist in a process of *exchange* with its milieu.

In the next chapter I will turn to Alfred North Whitehead's con-tribution to thinking the reversal of the hierarchy of mechanism over organism, where relations between organisms and whatever is external to them are constitutive of each organism and of the 'organic universe' as a whole. Our understanding of the relation between mechanism and finalism or purposeful process is described by both Whitehead and the complexity theorist Stuart Kauffman in terms of the bifurcation and reduction of reality for the purposes of analysis but with the unintended effect of omitting key aspects of the real: process, creativity and life.

NOTES

1. Canguilhem also points to the interdependency of terms such as monstros-ity or pathology and the importance of invention in the development of any science. In an essay on 'Monstrosity and the Monstrous', in *Knowledge of*

Life, a tension is discovered between what Canguilhem calls the Imaginary monstrous (what feeds creativity or invention) and a concrete monstrosity which ultimately brings cases of monstrosity under the system of natural law (i.e. there *are* no monsters in nature).

2. Georges Canguilhem, *Ideology and Rationality in the History of the Life Sciences* (Cambridge, MA: The MIT Press, 1988), p. 61.
3. Georges Canguilhem, 'Epistemology of Biology', in *A Vital Rationalist: Selected Writings from Georges Canguilhem* (New York: Zone Books, 2000), p. 68.
4. Canguilhem, *Knowledge of Life*, p. 5.
5. Ibid., pp. 5–6.
6. 'A history of science that views science as a progressive process of purification governed by *norms of verification* cannot fail to concern itself with scientific ideology. Gaston Bachelard distinguished between obsolete and valid science, and while it is wise to separate one from the other, it is also wise to study how the two are related. The obsolete is condemned in the name of truth and objectivity. But what is now obsolete was once considered objectively true. Truth must submit itself to criticism and possible refutation or there is no science' (Canguilhem, *Ideology and Rationality*, p. 39). See also Monica Greco, 'The Ambivalence of Error: "Scientific Ideology" in the History of the Life Sciences and Psychosomatic Medicine', *Social Science & Medicine*, 58, 2004, p. 689: 'The point worth noting, which gives us the key to many of the other features of Bachelard's thought, is that he presents the "structure of the mind" as dependent on science – it is shaped by science. This is the reason why a philosophy adequate for scientific thought cannot be a philosophy grounded in a metaphysical and unchanging faculty of reason, or in the subject understood as a given. Quite the reverse, reason is the product of science – not its raw material. Reason is instructed by science, in the sense that its objects and concepts are never immediate givens, but always objects and concepts that have already been produced through the work of science itself. In the most synthetic terms, Bachelard describes science as a form of work, a form of work mediated by instruments.'
7. Canguilhem, *Ideology and Rationality*, p. 38.
8. Ibid., p. 30.
9. Emmet Kennedy, 'Ideology from de Tracy to Marx', *Journal of the History of Ideas*, 40:3, 1979, pp. 353–68.
10. Ibid., pp. 354–5.
11. Ibid., p. 355.
12. Ibid., p. 357.
13. Canguilhem, *Ideology and Rationality*, p. 29.
14. Ibid., pp. 36–7; p. 105.
15. For example, regulation is respiration which produces heat; perspiration which cools; and digestion which restores to blood what is lost through respiration and perspiration.

16. Canguilhem, *Ideology and Rationality*, p. 108.
17. Ibid., p. 107.
18. Ibid., p. 115.
19. Ibid., p. 70.
20. Ibid., p. 117.
21. Ibid.
22. Ibid., p. 105.
23. Ibid., p. 118.
24. Canguilhem, *Knowledge of Life*, pp. 76–7.
25. Ibid., p. 80.
26. Ibid., p. 84; see also John Cottingham on a more subtle reading of Cartesian Dualism in '"A Brute to the Brutes?": Descartes' Treatment of Animals', *Philosophy*, 53, 1978, pp. 551–9.
27. Canguilhem, *Knowledge of Life*, p. 84.
28. Ibid., p. 87.
29. Ibid., p. 86.
30. Ibid., p. 88.
31. Ibid., p. 89.
32. Kurt Goldstein, *The Organism: A Holistic Approach to Biology Derived from Pathological Data in Man* (New York: Zone Books, 2000), pp. 84–5.
33. Ibid., pp. 333–4.
34. Cf. Canguilhem, *Ideology and Rationality*, p. 29: 'The *ideologues* ... proposed treating ideas as natural phenomena determined by the relation between man, a living, sensitive organism, and his natural environment.'
35. Maurice Merleau-Ponty, *The Phenomenology of Perception* (London: Routledge, 2002), p. 90.
36. Richard Dawkins, *The Extended Phenotype* (Oxford: Oxford University Press, 1982), p. 199.
37. Canguilhem, *Knowledge of Life*, pp. 96–7.
38. Donna Haraway, *Simians, Cyborgs and Women* (New York: Routledge, 1991), pp. 151–2.
39. Ibid., p. 152.
40. Katherine N. Hayles, *How We Became Posthuman: Virtual Bodies in Cybernetics, Literature and Informatics* (Chicago: University of Chicago Press, 1999), p. 115.
41. Haraway, *Simians, Cyborgs and Women*, pp. 149–50.
42. Ibid., p. 153.
43. Ibid., p. 154; see also Rosi Braidotti, 'Posthuman, All Too Human: Towards a New Process Ontology', *Theory Culture Society*, 23, 2006, p. 199: 'in her criticism of the exploitative logic of Western techno-sciences from within, Haraway (1997) stresses a number of crucial features. The first is power as a dynamic web of interconnections or hybrid contaminations, as a principle of radical non-purity. The second is the refusal to fall into the pitfall of the classical nature/culture divide: there is no natural *telos* or order, as distinct from technological mediation. In

order to restructure our collective relationship to the new nature/culture compound of contemporary techno-sciences, Haraway calls for a renewed kinship system, radicalised by concretely affectionate ties to the non-human "others".'

44. Braidotti, 'Posthuman, All Too Human', p. 198.
45. Haraway, *Simians, Cyborgs and Women*, p. 163.
46. Ibid., pp. 156–7.
47. Julia Kristeva, 'Women's Time', in Toril Moi (ed.), *The Kristeva Reader* (Oxford: Blackwell, 1986), p. 198.
48. Ibid.
49. Ibid.
50. Ibid., p. 199.
51. Ibid., p. 200.
52. Haraway, *Simians, Cyborgs and Women*, p. 176.
53. Ibid., p. 204.
54. Ibid., pp. 211–12.
55. Ibid., p. 218.

5. Organicism and Complexity: Whitehead and Kauffman

We saw how Canguilhem identified trends in the development of the life sciences towards concepts of non-life, and in Haraway's writings on the cyborg the movement towards information-based conceptions of organic function (the move from 'organism' to 'code'). The potential effects of these alternative modes of thinking animal life are twofold. On the one hand, animality becomes ever more subject or definable in terms that are essentially alien to a concept of life, facilitating our reduction of the lives of animals to mere mechanisms or instruments for our use. On the other hand, our understanding of the evolution of animal species points to the many and complex layers of kinship and symbiosis that have evolved across species lines, and the varied relationships that human beings form with other animals at an individual level require alternative expressions of the nature of *relation* itself. It is not enough to define human-animal interactions in terms of human psychology or moral categories if the very boundary between human and animal is continually shifting under the terms of the fast-developing life sciences.

This chapter, then, has several interrelated aims, the first of which is to continue to trace the reversals and reconfigurations of the hierarchy of the mechanical over the organic. In the writings of Whitehead, this will also involve a renewal of our thinking of relation in a reinscribed 'order of nature' built on original *processes* of 'unification' (organisms) rather than substances. Whitehead's thought, based on prehensive unification, which opens up many levels of description of the possible relations in which we are implicated, is intended to serve as a preface to Haraway's critique (and defence) of the sciences, and her analyses of the nature of human and animal interactions with science and technology. Through Stuart Kauffman's work, the aim is to promote a consideration of the specificity and irreducibility of biological processes, from the point of view of contemporary complexity theory as a modern acknowledgment of the limitations of evolutionary theories based purely on principles derived from physical laws, in common with Whitehead's criticisms of scientific method as overly reductive, which he sets out in *Science and the Modern World*. As Kauffman goes on to argue, organic evolution is irreducible to physics, in so far as it would require infinitely many simulations of evolutionary processes in order to model the development of life as it has occurred in this specific biosphere. We require instead an account of the emergence of biological systems, and the uniquely biological laws that govern life on earth (as well as the possible emergence of life elsewhere). Kauffman discusses a number of alternatives, but I will focus on his account of autocatalytic sets: that is, Kauffman's equivalent to Whitehead's account of the interdependence of parts in an organic whole.

MECHANICAL REDUCTION

Whitehead's arguments against what he characterises as scientific materialism, or the presupposition of 'the ultimate fact of an irreducible brute matter'[1] distributed throughout space, begin with the criticism of this concept of matter as senseless, valueless and purposeless. The challenge, which we also find in thinkers such as Henri Bergson and Georges Canguilhem, is to reverse the hierarchy in which materiality and mechanism precede and determine the organic. For Whitehead, this is not simply a case of according primacy to mind, spirit or the vital. Instead, Whitehead first attempts to illuminate the way in which two inconsistent attitudes have held sway in Western thought: first, a scientific realism based on mechanistic principles, and second, a belief in the sovereignty and self-determination of the human.[2]

To tackle the first of these in the context of a broader meditation on the advance of the sciences, and the relation this bears to metaphysical enquiry, Whitehead points to a number of fallacies committed in the course of scientific enquiry in particular, though these fallacies are by no means exclusive to any one field. The first of these, the fallacy of Simple Location, is described in *Science and the Modern World* as arising from the multifarious character of space-time. While things are commonly understood, and correctly in Whitehead's view, to be either separated or brought together in space and time (calling these the *separative* and *prehensive* characters of space-time – the significance of which I will return to shortly), Whitehead identifies a third character concerning the specificity or limitation of each thing in its shape and period of endurance. This individuality, or isolable character, of things Whitehead refers to as the *modal* character of space-time, and to focus on this aspect only, to the exclusion of the separative and prehensive characters, is the basis for the idea of simple location. As Whitehead outlines:

> To say that a bit of matter has *simple location* means that, in expressing its spatio-temporal relations, it is adequate to state that it is where it is, in a definite finite region of space, and throughout a definite finite duration of time, apart from any essential reference of the relations of that bit of matter to other regions of space and to other durations of time.[3]

Whitehead's contention will be that there are no elements of experience, as he goes on to analyse them, that have the characteristic of simple location. For our purposes, we will see in Whitehead's analysis of these 'primary elements' of experience the basis for an understanding of the development of the sciences as no longer 'physical' or 'biological' but as the study of *organisms*. The primary organisms (replacing the idea of purely biological phenomena that supplement physics as 'special cases', and thereby give rise to the problematic dualism of mechanism and vitalism) are not infinitely regressing (cells, atoms, particles, etc.), but are rather to be understood as *events*.[4]

Canguilhem (through Bichat and Bernard) showed us that mechanical description was insufficient for medical knowledge, the latter requiring a new concept and law of normal and pathological functioning. All pathology is consistent with physical law, and yet is detrimental to biological existence; that is, norms are relative to the particular optimal conditions particular to different organisms. More generally, as Ilya Prigogine explains in his study of historical formulations of the relation between physical determinism and 'indeterminacy' as the defining characteristic of living systems (or time reversibility and the seemingly irreversible moments of deviation that introduce aspects of creativity and life into material existence), the possibilities for its expression have been explored in both contemporary physics and philosophy. Prigogine cites attempts in the history of philosophy – by Kant, Heidegger and Whitehead – to rebuild the foundations of philosophical enquiry in order to address the insufficiency of deterministic physics in explaining fundamental aspects of human existence. For these philosophers, it is a 'tragic choice between an alienating science and an antiscientific philosophy'.[5] This choice manifests itself, for Whitehead, in the second fallacy he identifies as that of 'misplaced concreteness'. Citing the example of the distinction between Substance and qualities in seventeenth-century thought (e.g. Descartes and Locke), Whitehead bemoans the consequences of thinking nature as an indifferent material medium upon which the human mind projects the qualities of colour, sound, scent and so on. 'Thus nature gets credit which should in truth be reserved for ourselves: the rose for its scent: the nightingale for its song: the sun for its radiance.'[6]

Whitehead's particular response to the double thought of the mechanism of nature and the belief in human beings (and higher animals) as self-determining beings also leads him to a criticism of vitalism for the compromise that it makes with the mechanistic model. That is, mechanism is accepted as the model for all processes in inanimate nature, while the vitalist position 'holds that the mechanism is partially mitigated within living bodies'.[7] Merleau-Ponty has also contended, in his *Nature* lectures, that this compromise vitalism makes with mechanism locks the vitalist position (for example, in Bergson's *Creative Evolution*) into an insoluble, and ultimately unsatisfactory, dualism.[8]

Despite Whitehead's rejection of both mechanism and vitalism, he believes it is possible to address a recurring problem in the history of Western thought, which is that of the specificity of living processes against otherwise relatively predictable, law-governed processes in non-living matter. He observes, in *Process and Reality*, that:

> no biological science has been able to express itself apart from phraseology that is meaningless unless it refers to ideals proper to the organism in question. This aspect of the universe impressed itself on that great biologist and philosopher, Aristotle. His philosophy led to a wild overstressing of 'final causes' during the Christian middle ages; and thence, by reaction, to the correlative overstressing of the notion of 'efficient causes' during the modern scientific period.[9]

Whitehead's alternative, in contradistinction to vitalism, which does not go far enough in overturning mechanistic explanation, is an explanatory framework that functions equally well in accounting for the creative or self-reproducing qualities of living organisms and for non-living entities from electrons all the way up to geological systems: 'The doctrine which I am maintaining is that the whole concept of materialism only applies to very abstract entities, the product of logical discernment. The concrete enduring entities are organisms, so that the plan of the *whole* influences the very characters of the various subordinate organisms which enter into it.'[10] For example, in thinking the structure of a living organism, an electron inside its body is different to one outside its body; the plan of the whole organism modifies the plan of successive 'subordinate organisms' that make up that body alone. It is the 'principle of modification' that is general throughout nature, rather than the electrons (or other conceivable units) that make up material bodies. Whitehead acknowledges that, in the light of modern physics, there has been a development in physical explanation based on energy, which has already had the desired effect of displacing 'matter' as the fundamental 'substance'. However, he continues, 'energy is merely the name for the quantitative aspect of a structure of happenings; in short, it depends on the notion of the functioning of the organism'.[11] The challenge is to define organisms without reference to their spatial and material configurations in 'simple location'.

Whitehead goes on to note that it is necessary to think about processes (at a macroscopic level) such as the evolution of living organisms as themselves having the function of 'subordinate organisms' in relation to members of their own species, other competing species, and their physical environment. Thus, while it is useful to frame discussions of evolutionary development in terms of competition for resources, it is also necessary to consider the 'neglected side' of evolutionary machinery, that is, creativeness:

> The organisms can create their own environment. For this purpose, the single organism is almost helpless. The adequate forces require societies of cooperating organisms. But with such cooperation and in proportion to the effort put forward, the environment has a plasticity which alters the whole ethical aspect of evolution.[12]

Thus far, I have outlined how Whitehead describes the particular flaws arising from the belief in (mechanistic) materialism, such as the fallacies of misplaced concreteness and of simple location. I want to now turn to Whitehead's alternative to these 'products of logical discernment' which is an account of experience based on prehensions, made up of three elements: occasions, objective forms and subjective forms, which together describe reality, fundamentally, in terms of a network of *relations* (with prehensions occurring at all levels from molecules up to geological systems). We have seen, as broadly outlined in *Science and the Modern World*, that the real, for Whitehead, is irreducible to discrete objects (of a certain shape and duration), consisting instead of 'drops of becoming' (a phrase he borrows from William James) or, in other words, actual occasions or *events*.

To explain how these *events* are analysed in (and defended as the basis of) Whitehead's philosophy of organism, it is necessary to clarify a number of key definitions that he employs, primarily in two other significant works, *Process and Reality* (originally published in 1929) and *Adventures of Ideas* (1933). Whitehead sets out for himself the project of a speculative philosophy, the aim of which is:

> to frame a coherent, logical, necessary system of general ideas in terms of which every element of our experience can be interpreted. By this notion of 'interpretation' I mean that everything of which we are conscious, as enjoyed, perceived, willed, or thought, shall have the character of a particular instance of the general scheme.[13]

As with thinkers such as Kant and Bergson in their earlier attempts to reconcile philosophy and science, the task of philosophy is defined against the perceived methods and aims of scientific enquiry. For Whitehead, against the abstractions (useful, but partial or perspectival) of science, the philosopher's endeavour is to 'work at the concordance of ideas conceived as illustrated in the concrete facts of the real world. It seeks those generalities which characterise the complete reality of fact.'[14] In *The Concept of Nature* (1920), Whitehead describes the advance of human thought in terms of the enactment of a fundamental division that has served to accelerate the divergence of the fields of philosophy and science. This fundamental division results in two orders of experience: on the one hand, we have 'conceptual' entities such as electrons as studied by the physicist, and on the other hand, 'observational' apprehensions of nature, or the 'byplay of the mind'.[15] Whitehead refers to this as 'the bifurcation of nature', and its overriding result is that enquiry tends to be focused on no more than either 'conjecture' or 'dream'. The not inconsiderable aim of the speculative philosophy is thus to cast off any notions of an *apparent* nature and, as stated above, lay down a *system of general ideas in terms of which every element of our experience can be interpreted.* What these elements consist of precisely (and, in the next chapter, we will see how they are used by Haraway to rethink common divisions between species, genders and other 'kinds'), requires, for Whitehead, a return to philosophy 'before Kant', from Plato to the early modern empiricists, in order to consider experience before the Copernican Revolution that placed the human subject at the centre of nature.

THE ORDER OF NATURE

A number of general features of Whitehead's project are outlined in the early pages of *Process and Reality*. Whitehead compares his philosophy to that of Spinoza (albeit a Spinoza mediated through the work of Samuel Alexander), pointing to many similarities between them, with the exception of the subject-predicate form of thought: 'The result is that the "substance-quality" concept is avoided; and that morphological description is replaced by description of dynamic process.'[16] Process, not some absolute (substance or God, or some other higher order reality), is the 'ultimate' to which all of its accidental embodiments refer. Furthermore, the difficulty of thinking process as the ultimate basis of things is compounded by the limitations of linguistic expression. Propositions, as philosophy's equivalent to scientific instruments, must, in the attempt to express general ideas, not only refer to a single fact (and we have already seen that there is no such thing is a 'simply located' object), but each one must also: 'propose the general character of the universe required for that fact ... A proposition can embody partial truth because it only demands a certain type of systematic environment, which is presupposed in its meaning. It does not refer to the universe in all its detail.'[17] In expressing the *general character of the universe* (making any particular fact 'what it is'), or its *organic reality*, we would be doing so at one of two levels, which give us two senses in which Whitehead uses the term 'organism' in his speculative scheme.

First of all, the 'microscopic' meaning of organism is 'concerned with the formal constitution of an actual occasion, considered as a process of realising an individual unit of experience'.[18] At the 'macroscopic' level (which we can compare to Sartre's discussion of the significance of taking one's facticity into account in *Being and Nothingness*), we would be

> concerned with the givenness of the actual world, considered as the stubborn fact which at once limits and provides opportunity for the actual occasion. The canalisation of the creative urge, exemplified in its mass reproduction of social nexūs, is for common sense the final illustration of the power of stubborn fact. Also in our experience, we essentially arise out of our bodies which are the stubborn facts of the immediate relevant past.[19]

To undertake these different levels of organic description is to recommence philosophical thinking in accordance with an order of nature based on the fundamental unit we have identified so far: events or processes. Once we have granted that the basis of all things (or rather all that we traditionally refer to as 'things') is process, we can see the consequences of this processive account of nature for our understanding of each of the elements that constitute experience. In common with the philosophy of Henri Bergson, Whitehead's philosophy of organism factors in the formation of individual subjectivity and consciousness as by-products of the creativity of the universe (this creativity simply being the universe 'making itself', to use Bergson's phrase):

> All knowledge is conscious discrimination of objects experienced. But this conscious discrimination, which is knowledge, is nothing more than an additional factor in the subjective form of the interplay of subject with object. This interplay is the stuff constituting those individual things which make up the sole reality of the Universe.[20]

We start, then, not with consciousness, but with the 'interplay' that describes the *relation* between the perceiver (which is not necessarily human, nor indeed living or biological) and perceived, that is, we commence with the ultimate real things (relations), which Whitehead names 'actual entities' (used interchangeably with 'actual occasions' or, as I have referred to them above, 'events'). Whitehead reminds us that we need to keep in mind that the focus is on the smallest possible time-spans (perhaps of a fraction of second), and that anything that can be 'experienced' qualifies as an actual occasion:

> The Aristotelian doctrine, that all agency is confined to actuality, is accepted. So also is the Platonic dictum that the very meaning of existence is 'to be a factor in agency', or in other words 'to make a difference'. Thus, 'to be something' is to be discoverable as a factor in the analysis of some actuality. It follows that in one sense everything is 'real', according to its own category of being.[21]

Central to Whitehead's entire philosophical scheme is his description of the precise manner in which actual occasions are connected to one another. As we have seen, the relations between actualities or events are not determined by a conscious or knowing subject, but simply by any entity that is capable of 'taking account of' another entity. Whitehead recalls Leibniz's distinction, in terms of generality, between perception and apperception, where *apperception* refers to the way in which higher monads take account of other monads. In a similar vein, Whitehead distinguishes between the terms *apprehension* and *prehension*, where the latter designates a 'taking account of' that is tied neither to consciousness nor to representative perception.[22] Now, the relations between actual occasions in prehensions also have a 'vector' character. In other philosophical phraseology, we might call this vector character 'intentionality' or perhaps even 'telos', in so far as prehensions involve some emotion, intention or aim, though the overriding definition of the directionality of prehensions essentially refers to the relations between past, present and future.[23] In this respect, prehensions start to give us the rudiments of subjectivity, though this is qualified by the way in which prehensions can attain relative subject or object status (that is, each prehension can be an object for another prehension). This now allows the analysis of prehensions into three elements: the occasion of activity, the datum or object, and the subjective form or 'affective tone' of that occasion.[24] Together, these elements, and the entire web of connections that is constructed through the process of prehensive unification, form Whitehead's doctrine of Immanence:

> This is at once the doctrine of the unity of Nature, and of the unity of each human life. The conclusion follows that our consciousness of the self-identity pervading our life-thread of occasions, is nothing other than knowledge of a special strand of unity within the general unity of nature. It is a locus within the whole, marked out by its own peculiarities, but otherwise exhibiting the general principle which guides the constitution of the whole. This general principle is the object-to-subject structure of experience. It can be otherwise

stated as the vector-structure of nature. Or otherwise, it can be conceived as the doctrine of the immanence of the past energising in the present.[25]

In the passage above, a number of key points are reiterated: first, the structure that informs nature is the same structure and unity that informs human, and all other, life (organic unity occurs all the way down); second, in resonance with certain readings of Bergson's theory of ontological memory,[26] Whitehead's scheme recognises human intention and creativity as an instance within a wider process (the creativity of Nature); and third, subjectivity is emergent.

The theory of prehensions forms the core of the philosophy of organism and, as Whitehead notes, all description apart from the processes of prehensive unification are forms of abstraction. When Whitehead goes on to elaborate on a range of other specialist terms in his philosophy, they are merely qualifications of the prehensive relations described above. In this vein, the remainder of this section on the philosophy of organism will be concerned with a more detailed consideration of the ways in which 'process' operates as its ontological basis. The distinction that Whitehead makes between *concrescence* and *transition* is central to this description of process, and it is made in order to account for our common ascriptions of permanence (or endurance) and change to things, and for the prevalence in the history of philosophy of the posing of a fundamental opposition between an ontologically prior enduring substance and the changes, accidents and diminutions that this substance 'suffers'. The definitions of concrescence and transition, on the other hand, are designed to express the uniqueness of actual entities (there is no general order, only order peculiar to each actual entity), the irreducible multiplicity of relations between entities, and yet to invoke a general framework within which all processes unfold.

For Whitehead, the process of concrescence is the manner in which all things 'become what they are'; it is the trajectory or vector that the actual entities follow. It then 'terminates with the attainment of a fully *determinate* "satisfaction"; and the creativity thereby passes over into the "given" primary phase for the concrescence of other actual entities'.[27] This passage from a determinate satisfaction (a completed object) into another concrescence of prehensions is termed 'Transition'; that is, the process by which a thing (animal, vegetable or mineral) becomes 'object' for something or someone else. Whitehead summarises the relation between the two aspects of process in the following passage:

An instance of concrescence is termed 'actual entity' – or equivalently, an 'actual occasion.' There is not one completed set of things which are actual occasions. For the fundamental inescapable fact is the creativity in virtue of which there can be no 'many things' which are not subordinated in a concrete unity. Thus a set of actual occasions is by the nature of things a standpoint for another concrescence which elicits a concrete unity from those many actual occasions. Thus we can never survey the actual world except from the standpoint of an immediate concrescence which is falsifying the presupposed completion. The creativity in virtue of which any relative complete actual world is, by the nature of things, the datum for a new concrescence is termed 'transition.' Thus, by reason of transition, 'the actual world' is always a relative term, and refers to that basis of presupposed actual occasions which is a datum for the novel concrescence.[28]

We can break down Whitehead's scheme in the following way, adding to this the distinction between microscopic and macroscopic description mentioned above:

(a) Microscopic process

- Instead of an enduring individual substance, there is a concrescence of actual occasions. Concrescence describes what would otherwise be called the permanence, relative endurance or *identity* of entities.
- No 'thing' (actual occasion) is complete, but rather always in process (the ultimate basis of all things is process, not substance).
- All multiplicities come under some sort of unity (organic structure works all the way up).

(b) Macroscopic process

- In order to apprehend any 'thing' in particular, we effect an artificial isolation (petrification) of the process ('falsifying the presupposed completion').
- The process of a falsely completed set of events (actual entities) becoming 'object' for another concrescence is called 'transition'. Transition is the process of becoming-other: a movement from the actual present to the 'merely real' but not yet actual or instantiated future. Transition describes the way in which all entities can be subordinated to the forces, influence or thoughts of other entities.

In the accounts of concrescence and transition, Whitehead emphasises the subjective character of prehensions, but also emphasises that the philosophy of organism is intended to provide an alternative to (indeed, a reversal of) Kant's analysis of the subject-based conditions of possible experience from which emerges what we commonly think of as the objective world. Whitehead's alternative is to commence with a description of the objective world, and then from it the emergence of the *superject*. To elaborate on what he means by the term 'superject',

Whitehead outlines the 'threefold character' of an actual entity: '(i) it has the character 'given' for it by the past; (ii) it has the subjective character aimed at in its process of concrescence; (iii) it has the superjective character, which is the pragmatic value of its specific satisfaction qualifying the transcendent creativity'.[29] To reiterate, the term 'satisfaction' is used to denote an actual entity at the end or outcome of its process of concrescence. It has become concrete, and objectified for another entity, and thus is emergent as *superject*, rather than fundamental or grounding in the way that either substance or subject is understood to be.

In the terms explained so far, an actual entity can exist in relation to any other actual entity, and thereby make up a prehension, be it the prehensions of a rocky cliff eroding by action of the wind and sea, or the prehensions of a herbivorous animal grazing in a field. The 'subjects' of these prehensions are of only latter significance, having emerged only subsequently as the results of the coalescence of actual entities into relatively unified prehensions and nexūs.[30] In order to think about the processes of prehensive unification at the level of individuals to which we might ascribe consciousness or conscious intentions, we need to turn to Whitehead's discussion of the emergence and operation of 'societies'. A society is 'self-sustaining':

> To constitute a society, the class-name has got to apply to each member, by reason of genetic derivation from other members of that same society. The members of the society are alike because, by reason of their common character, they impose on other members of the society the conditions which lead to that likeness.[31]

The description here is now at the level of 'persons' or 'conscious subjects': Whitehead provides the example of the life of a man, which is composed of a historical progression or interaction of actual entities, each of which could be said to 'inherit' from one another. It is in this sense that we would consider this man to be 'the same enduring person from birth to death'.[32] Societies can possess different degrees of order, and different phases of one person's life can each constitute a distinct society, with reference to whatever defining characteristic constitutes order in that society. Whitehead uses the example of the acquisition of a language. To use an example from my own life, at the age of six, I started to take lessons in reading Arabic; in the 'society' that I understand to be the historical route of my life this would constitute a subordinate society in reference to knowledge of the Arabic language. The eventual loss of my ability to understand Arabic, due to lack of practice, marks the end of that society (with reference to Arabic), but I can still be said, by virtue of a complex collection of other enduring characteristics, to be one and the same individual. This latter sense of a human individual as a society gains its unity from a certain 'personal order',[33] but as Whitehead reminds us, in this description based on the procession of actual entities, nothing is completely what it is until it belongs to the past. That is, when it is in existence in the present it is still in the process of becoming what it is: 'Until the death of the man and the destruction of the earth, there is no determinate nexus which in an unqualified sense is either the man or the earth.'[34] In line with the organic structure of all levels of interaction of actual entities, prehensions, and nexūs, all societies only exist and function within a web of adjacent societies, to different degrees of dependency or relevance. At this level, we start to see affinities between the philosophy of organism and Merleau-Ponty's account of embodied subjectivity and intersubjectivity, and embeddedness within one's environment as a factor in the constitution of experience.

In his subsequent discussions of the characteristics of living societies, and what we understand to be 'life' in general, Whitehead adheres to a somewhat common conception of the relation between human and non-human life:

> when we survey the living world, animal and vegetable, there are bodies of all types. Each living body is a society, which is not personal. But most of the animals, including all the vertebrates, seem to have their social system dominated by a subordinate society which is 'personal'. This subordinate society is of the same type as 'man', according to the personal definition given above, though of course the mental poles in the occasions of the dominant personal society do not rise to the height of human mentality. Thus in one sense a dog is a 'person', and in another sense he is a non-personal society.[35]

The broad definition of life, for Whitehead, is simply 'reaction adapted to the capture of intensity, under a large variety of circumstances. But the reaction is dictated by the present and not the past. It is the clutch at vivid immediacy.'[36] Despite the similarities between Whitehead and Bergson on many counts, such as their identification of the intellectual tendency towards spatialisation, and the basis of reality in 'process', this definition of life is relatively underdeveloped in Whitehead's writings compared to the complex interlinking of concepts of creativity, memory and organic evolution that Bergson delineates through his main works, *Matter and Memory* and *Creative Evolution*, as we saw in Chapters 1 and 2. However, Whitehead's endeavour to explain the emergence of unifying control in living bodies, as opposed, for example, to the *dissociation* of cells from an original substance, underlines that the sense of 'personal order' used above is ontologically anterior to the formation of relations at the level of pre-human or pre-individual actual entities. There are, as Whitehead observes, centres of reaction and control in nature which cannot be identified with a centre of experience, that is, consciousness (the various forms of vegetative life provide such examples of non-personal order).[37] Brian Henning uses the Whiteheadian view of individuality as irreducible to substance or essence, pointing instead to its basis in societies of actual entities or 'community' (e.g. a plant is a community of cells, each of which is itself a community), to promote an alternative environmental and animal ethic. Animals are not like rocks (which are simply aggregates, in Whitehead's terms) but are communities, and all communities deserve moral consideration. Thus moral consideration can be extended to all living things which are communities, a view which aligns with that of the 'intrinsic value' of subjects-of a-life in the writings of Tom Regan, for example.[38]

In summary, Whitehead's philosophy of organism attempts to bridge (or perhaps circumvent) the gulf between materialism and vitalism by describing systems (physical, chemical, biological, psychological, etc.) through what he admits is, in many ways, a Spinozist formulation of relations at a sub- or pre-individual level. It is a system of relations that seeks to account for the emergence of life and creativity, with a particular recognition of the plasticity of relation between the parts within a single organism, and indeed between organisms and their environment.

THE SPECIFICITY OF BIOLOGY

We have seen how Whitehead ultimately provides a way of decomposing and recomposing all levels of experience (so seemingly susceptible to reductionist abstraction, but necessarily mindful of this potential, hence the fallacies of misplaced concreteness and simple location) while also granting real status to elements of experience that tend to be disregarded, at least in more reductionist schemes. The effort to overcome mechanical explanation (mechanics as physics) shows that the hierarchy of mechanical over organic in terms of ontological priority is far from decisive. I want now to turn to the work of the biologist and complexity theorist, Stuart Kauffman, for his presentation of arguments for the natural or expected emergence of life as a property of the physical world. As Stengers notes,[39] Kauffman's theoretical approach is an attempt to state the specificity of life, and the need to formulate specifically biological laws in addition to the known laws of physics, in the terms of physics itself. In this respect, Kauffman shares with Whitehead a resistance to a return to vitalism, but also dissatisfaction with the terms of the physical sciences in the description of living processes.

Kauffman's project, reformulated across a number of works, takes as its starting point the problem of physical reductionism, arguing in

Reinventing the Sacred (2008) that evolutionary processes cannot be reduced to physics alone, either epistemologically or ontologically. That is, we cannot deduce upwards from the base of physics to the specific evolution of our biosphere, nor can we rely on physics to determine what count as real entities: reductionist physics dictates that all things, or real entities, are particles in motion.[40] On both counts, the physicist's explanations for the emergence of the diversity particular to our biosphere would have to involve the selection and prediction of the trajectories of such a huge number of genetic and environmental changes that 'they would have to carry out infinitely many . . . simulations in order to model our specific biosphere with perfect precision'.[41] Thus, rather than attempting to start from the base of physical laws, Kauffman will argue that it must be acknowledged that biology is both epistemologically and ontologically emergent.[42]

The arguments against the reductionist approach hinge on the use of different orders of language, or language games as Kauffman, taking his cue from Wittgenstein, calls them.[43] Essentially, two levels or language games are in operation when attempting to reduce living processes to physics. Here, Kauffman echoes Whitehead's identification, as discussed above, of the problem of the bifurcation of nature in which the universe is variously described in terms of either the perceived world (the byplay of the mind) or in terms of theoretical physics (at the level of protons and electrons). As with Whitehead's project, Kauffman's aim to find the laws that govern all possible life (terrestrial and non-terrestrial) should not simply supplement the existing laws of physics, making biology only a 'special case' in relation to otherwise physically lawful processes (as we saw, Whitehead rejected vitalism for reinforcing this model). Rather, Kauffman suggests that such biological laws will, in fact, not only complement but also serve to alter our understanding of physics.[44]

In the following section, I will go through a number of the key elements of Kauffman's project, in his works *At Home in the Universe* (1995), *Investigations* (2000), *and Reinventing the Sacred* (2008), in which questions concerning the reduction of complex biological organisation to physics (or mechanics) are addressed.

Historically, attempts to theorise the creation of life have tended to rest on the assumption that it is either simply a phenomenon that can, at some future point, be reduced to existing finite physical models, or that it is some extraordinarily mysterious and elusive event that can only be described in the form of a metaphor or cryptic image. For an example of the latter, Kauffman repeatedly makes reference to the image of an *élan vital* (or vital impulse), as the archetype of the vitalist theory of a 'central directing agency' responsible for the formation of living organisms.[45] Kauffman notes that the lineage (which I discussed in Chapter 1) from August Weismann's theory of the germ-plasm to modern biology's focus on the structure of DNA has been dominated by a view of life as having some form of central directing agency, whereas Kant had earlier expressed the idea of organisms as autopoietic wholes 'in which each part existed both for and by means of the whole, while the whole existed for and by means of the parts'.[46] It is this earlier sense of an autopoietic whole that is re-invigorated in Kauffman's theory of the interactions of 'autonomous agents' composed of, and themselves forming, autocatalytic sets. The intention is thus not to focus on the vehicle of hereditary transmission, which was the founding, but not fully formulated, assumption of Darwin's *Origin of Species*. Rather it is to provide a theory of the conditions necessary for the very emergence of life in the first place, one possible theory being that of collectively autocatalytic sets in which 'there is no central directing agency. There is no separate genome, no DNA. There is a collective molecular autopoietic system.'[47] The term *élan vital* is, of course, attributable to Henri Bergson but, as we shall see, the alternative model of the emergence and processes of life will look remarkably similar to the models of creative process that both Bergson and Whitehead propose as alternatives to mechanistic reduction. As Kauffman goes on to state, in unintentionally Bergsonian terms: 'the emergence of self-reproducing molecular systems may be highly probable. No small conclusion this: Life abundant, emergent, expected. Life spattered across megaparsecs, galaxies, galactic clusters. We as members of a creative, mysteriously unfolding universe.'[48] Instead of having recourse to the equally insufficient alternatives of reductionism and vitalism, Kauffman commences with the simple acknowledgement of the abundance or ubiquity of life, or ways of making a living that, at a minimum, can be based on the work cycles of what he will term 'autonomous agents':

> What is happening in a biosphere is that autonomous agents are coconstructing and propagating organisations of work, of constraint construction, and of task completion that continue to propagate and proliferate diversifying organisation.
>
> This statement is just plain true. Just look out your windows, burrow down a foot or so, and try to establish what all the microscopic life is busy doing and building and has done for billions of years, let alone the macroscopic ecosystem of plants, herbivores, and carnivores that is slipping, sliding, hiding, hunting, bursting with flowers and leaves outside your window.[49]

Thinking about these processes in terms of the actions of autonomous agents thus forms the basis for a concept of 'propagating organisation' that should constitute the foundations of living processes in general. For Kauffman, the *minimal molecular autonomous agent* (the simplest manifestation of agency) is an agent that can act on its own behalf in an environment, and to which it is appropriate to attribute a certain teleology: 'When biologists talk of a bacterium swimming up a glucose gradient "to get" sugar, they are using teleological language. But we would not say a ball was rolling "to get" downhill . . . Let us stretch and say it is appropriate to apply it to the bacterium. We may do so without attributing consciousness to the bacterium.'[50] Again with an allusion to Wittgenstein's theory of language games, Kauffman employs the term 'natural games' to describe the different modes of 'making a living' that are available to organisms in the biosphere. These natural games are 'searched for' in the processes of mutation and recombination of DNA, and thus successful variations of making a living will come to populate a biosphere over the course of time.[51] Autonomous agents, playing these natural games, will, across generations, continue to proliferate in novel directions at all levels (molecular, morphological, behavioural, organisational), and it is this 'push' into novelty that Kauffman will express in terms of the mathematical concept of an 'adjacent possible' which I will discuss at the end of this section.[52]

What sort of systems might autonomous agents be? Or, as Kauffman asks, 'What must a physical system be such that it can act on its own behalf in an environment?'[53] Recall that, in the absence of any central directing agency, the theory of autocatalytic sets as the basis for the emergence of life is proposed instead as a 'collective molecular autopoietic system'. In this scheme, life could simply be a natural property arising from complex chemical systems:

> when the number of different kinds of molecules in a chemical soup passes a certain threshold, a self-sustaining network of reactions – an autocatalytic metabolism – will suddenly appear. Life emerged, I suggest, not simple, but complex and whole, and has remained complex and whole ever since . . . thanks to the simple, profound transformation of dead molecules into an organisation by which each molecule's formation is catalysed by some other molecule in the organisation.[54]

Kauffman goes on to set out the key elements of the process described above: catalysis, autocatalytic 'loops', and phase transition, all in the context of an overarching 'nonergodic' or non-repeating quality of natural processes (the model of possibility operant in Kauffman's suggested theory of life's creativity).

Autocatalysis is, at its simplest, a system of chemical reactions in which the molecules contained in that system are capable of catalysing their own reproduction. The catalysts we are probably most familiar with are digestive enzymes which help to speed up the breakdown of the foods that we ingest into their component parts to enable their absorption and use by our bodies. An *auto*catalytic system 'is one in which the molecules speed up the very reactions by which they themselves are formed: A makes B; B makes C; C makes A again.'[55] In fact, every living organism, put simply, constitutes a complex set of thousands of these autocatalytic loops or reactions. The constitution of these autocatalytic loops is termed the achievement of catalytic closure, and this, for Kauffman, is essentially the definition of life. In order for life to arise, under this definition, all that would be required is that some of the component molecules in a system can act as both ingredient in the reactions and as catalyst to speed up the reactions in that collection. (As Kauffman observes, there are already molecules, such as ribozomes, a type of RNA, and the enzyme trypsin, that have this dual property):

> A set of molecules either does or does not have the property of catalytic closure. Catalytic closure means that every molecule in the system either is supplied from the outside as "food" or is itself synthesised by reactions catalysed by molecular species within the autocatalytic system. Catalytic closure is not mysterious. But it is not a property of any single molecule; it is a property of a system of molecules. It is an emergent property.[56]

While many naturally occurring, and synthesised, collections of chemical reactions amongst 'dead' molecules have been observed, the moment at which a system of chemical reactions achieves catalytic closure has yet to be synthesised in a laboratory, although Kauffman speculates that this may be possible within a few decades.[57]

Kauffman draws a number of conclusions from this speculative look at the possibilities for thinking the origin of life: while such self-sustaining systems can be simulated by human beings, they are not yet self-reproducing, that is, we have not succeeded in creating life in a laboratory, but at least some doubt has been thrown on the idea that life is driven or defined by a central directing agency.[58] If life was originally created in this relatively simple process of accumulating systems of catalytic closure, then life may well have arisen from 'non-life' and 'life is vastly more probable than we have supposed. Not only are we at home in the universe, but we are far more likely to share it with as yet unknown companions.'[59]

Having identified the minimally active components of living systems, autonomous agents, which may be composed of autocatalytic sets, as described above, the final contention of Kauffman's that I want to discuss is that such sets or systems, once they come into being (for example, by achieving catalytic closure), constitute processes, over the course of their own lives and those of successive generations, that constantly explode into their 'adjacent possibles'. This movement, by adjustments in behaviour and responsiveness to the environment, will essentially form the 'arrow of time' for living systems. Returning to the rejection of physical reductionism, Kauffman argues that the Darwinian account of the emergence of 'preadaptions' cannot simply be stated in terms of calculable probabilities. The formation of such changes did not arise probabilistically: it would not have been possible to 'play out' the requisite number of formations in the time that life has actually taken to unfold in our universe.[60] Rather, the evolution of molecules and species in the biosphere is vastly nonrepeating or, using the physicist's technical term, *nonergodic*.[61] It is thus asked whether it might be necessary to formulate new laws, in addition to the three laws of thermodynamics that govern the directionality of self-constructing systems that constitute biological evolution.[62] As we said above, the explosion of forms of life into their adjacent possibles could be thought of as the arrow of time for living systems. As Kauffman defines it, the adjacent possible 'consists of all those molecular species that are not members of the actual, but are *one reaction step away from the actual*'.[63] Or, in other words, those new molecular species that 'can be synthesised from the actual molecular species in a single reaction step from substrates in the actual to products in the adjacent possible'.[64]

Against the 'ergodic' model of nature in which the universe moves towards equilibrium, life poses a particular problem: 'For equilibrium with respect to all macroscopic properties to have been attained, it is not necessary that all microstates have been sampled, of course, but that the statistical distribution of microstates approaches the equilibrium distribution.'[65] Another way of stating this is that in order for the development of life to have proceeded 'lawfully', in a way that we could simulate and therefore predict, all of the possible combinations of amino acid chains (of length 200, for example), would had to have been 'sampled' in order for the currently existent set of proteins to have been selected from this range. However, as Kauffman points out: 'It would take at least 10 to 67th times the current lifetime of the universe for the universe to manage to make all possible proteins of length 200 at least once. Obviously, with respect to proteins of length 200 the universe is vastly nonergodic. It cannot have equilibrated over all these possible different molecules.'[66] Thus, the effort to conceive of dedicated laws of biology reinvigorates the vitalist intuition of the specificity of the living (there is another, supra-mechanical, order of selection operating in the evolution of life), but Kauffman's speculations seek to reshape the laws of physics themselves in the realisation of both the limitations and possibilities of scientific explanation.

To conclude, an engagement with Whitehead's philosophy of organism provides us with an understanding of relation (radically empirical, in James' sense) that allows us to think all levels of reality, and potentially infinite kinds of combinations or conjunctions otherwise precluded by more abstract categorisations of reality, especially of the living. At a microscopic level, things that we normally assume to be whole or integral are really disaggregated, such as the sense of my own personhood or subjectivity which is in fact fragmented into prehensions. At a macroscopic level (or the level at which our subjective agency actually comes to operate as 'societies' of prehensions) we are connected to things that we ordinarily think of as being dissociated from us, such as the lives of animals that we dispose of for food, labour or experimentation.

Where Haraway, in 'The Cyborg Manifesto', sees the 'end' or terminal point of the process of the devitalisation of life in the dominance of information systems, Kauffman's complexity theory reinforces in more recent terms, from within the life sciences, the specificity of biological processes. This will raise questions for us, in the next chapter, about the consistency of this scientific acknowledgement of the specificity of life with the modern application of proprietary models (e.g. the patenting of genetically modified organisms) to living things, as if human *interventions* could now count as *inventions*. Having seen the arguments against mechanism as a form of reductionism, the reduction of any living organism (which is still self-generating, in the strictest sense) to human artifice seems premature. Indeed, we will see that this has proven to be a contentious issue in the case of the patent granted in the US for the OncoMouse. The next chapter will explore the implications of this contradictory status that animals still possess in the context of the life sciences.

NOTES

1. Alfred North Whitehead, *Science and the Modern World* (New York: The Free Press, [1925] 1967), p. 17.
2. Ibid., p. 76.
3. Ibid., p. 58.
4. Ibid., pp. 102–3.
5. Ilya Prigogine, *The End of Certainty* (New York: The Free Press, 1997), p. 10.
6. Whitehead, *Science and the Modern World*, p. 54.
7. Ibid., p. 79.
8. Maurice Merleau-Ponty, *La Nature: Notes, Cours de Collège de France* (Paris: Seuil, 1994).

9. Alfred North Whitehead, *Process and Reality* (New York: The Free Press, [1929] 1978), p. 84.
10. Whitehead, *Science and the Modern World*, p. 79.
11. Ibid., p. 102
12. Ibid., pp. 111–12.
13. Whitehead, *Process and Reality*, p. 3.
14. Whitehead, *Adventures of Ideas*, p. 146.
15. Alfred North Whitehead, *The Concept of Nature* (New York: Prometheus Books, [1920] 2004), pp. 30–1.
16. Whitehead, *Process and Reality*, p. 7.
17. Ibid., p. 11.
18. Ibid., p. 129.
19. Ibid.
20. Whitehead, *Adventures of Ideas*, p. 177.
21. Ibid., p. 197.
22. Ibid., pp. 233–4.
23. Whitehead, *Process and Reality*, p. 19.
24. Whitehead, *Adventures of Ideas*, p. 174.
25. Ibid., p. 187.
26. See the final chapter of Bergson's *Matter and Memory*, and Gilles Deleuze's reading in *Le Bergsonisme* (Paris: Presses Universitaires de France, 1966) of Bergson's *Creative Evolution* and *Matter and Memory* as texts that together constitute a monistic, ontological theory of memory.
27. Whitehead, *Process and Reality*, p. 85.
28. Ibid., p. 211.
29. Ibid., p. 87.
30. A collection of prehensions is called a *nexus*, or plural *nexūs*. The togetherness of nexūs then make up the whole range of 'objects' that are familiar to us in common language: e.g. regions, societies, persons, enduring objects, corporal substances, living organisms (Whitehead, *Adventures of Ideas*, p. 198).
31. Whitehead, *Process and Reality*, p. 89.
32. Ibid., p. 90.
33. Ibid.
34. Whitehead, *Adventures of Ideas*, p. 204.
35. Ibid., pp. 205–6.
36. Whitehead, *Process and Reality*, p. 105.
37. See Whitehead, *Process and Reality*, p. 108. This compares readily to Bergson's account of emergent subjectivity in the first chapter of *Matter and Memory*: the emergence and coalescence of centres of real action, surrounded by a zone of indetermination. In *Process and Reality*, p. 108, Whitehead explains that the mind-body problem emerges from a misunderstanding of the relations between the physical and mental poles of actual entities.
38. Brian Henning, *The Ethics of Creativity: Beauty, Morality and Nature in*

a Processive Cosmos (Pittsburgh: University of Pittsburgh Press, 2005). Henning's use of Whitehead's work is extremely comprehensive, but limits its philosophical engagement to the well-known links between Whitehead and the American Pragmatists (Dewey, James, Peirce), and to established moral philosophy; for example, Whiteheadian morality as the achievement of beauty is compared to Aldo Leopold's land ethic. Daniel A. Dombrowski, in *Hartshorne and the Metaphysics of Animal Rights* (New York: SUNY Press, 1988), turns to another process philosopher, Charles Hartshorne, to promote the study of metaphysics in order to think about the treatment of animals, in particular process metaphysics for its alternative to (Kantian) formulations of sovereign subjectivity and individuality. The 'pre-individual' process approach of Hartshorne is put forward in order to resolve the dispute between the environmentalist focus on species and ecosystems and the animal rights focus on individuals.

39. Isabelle Stengers, *Thinking with Whitehead: A Free and Wild Creation of Concepts* (Cambridge, MA: Harvard University Press, 2011), p. 331.
40. Stuart Kauffman, *Reinventing the Sacred: A New View of Science, Reason, and Religion* (New York: Basic Books, 2008), p. 3.
41. Ibid., p. 39.
42. Ibid.
43. Stuart Kauffman, *Investigations* (Oxford: Oxford University Press, 2000), p. 51.
44. Kauffman, *Reinventing The Sacred*, p. 45.
45. Kauffman, *Investigations*, p. 8.
46. Stuart Kauffman, *At Home in the Universe* (Oxford: Oxford University Press, 1995), p. 274.
47. Ibid., p. 275.
48. Kauffman, *Investigations*, p. 16.
49. Ibid., p. 5.
50. Kauffman, *Reinventing The Sacred*, p. 78.
51. Kauffman, *Investigations*, p. 75.
52. See Kauffman, *Investigations*, p. 150: Kauffman even makes a reference to cells possibly 'prehending' their chemically adjacent possible (though acknowledges that this risks heading into the realm of consciousness/mind on matter relations).
53. Kauffman, *Investigations*, p. 8.
54. Kauffman, *At Home in the Universe*, pp. 47–8.
55. Ibid., p. 49.
56. Ibid., p. 275.
57. Ibid., p. 58. Kauffman speculates that the phenomenon of 'phase transition' could be the basis for the emergence of complex living systems, or the point at which catalytic closure is achieved: 'The analogue in the origin-of-life theory will be that when a large enough number of reactions are catalysed in a chemical reaction system, a vast web of catalysed reac-

tions will suddenly crystallise. Such a web, it turns out, is almost certainly autocatalytic – almost certainly self-sustaining, alive.'

58. Kauffman, *At Home in the Universe* p. 66; p. 275.
59. Ibid., p. 69.
60. Kauffman, *Reinventing The Sacred*, p. 130.
61. Ibid., p. 120.
62. Kauffman, *Investigations*, p. 142.
63. Ibid.
64. Ibid. One might compare the configuration of the adjacent possible to that of virtual objects in Bergson's model of memory: that is, along with the actual object perceived, a set of virtual or possible actions is given with the object, such that there is no clean division between subject or agent and object. There is instead a complex relation that is entered into constituting the minimum unit of any experience (be it of a block of potassium in contact with water, up to an animal encountering a source of food). As Whitehead states, the minimum instance of being is a relation, a process.
65. Kauffman, *Investigations*, p. 141.
66. Kauffman, *Investigations*, p. 144; 'Furthermore, many proteins are of length 300 or up to 1000 amino acids. Thus even proceeding along the Planck timescale (10^{-43} seconds), it would take the universe 10^{39} its current lifetime to synthesise all proteins of length 200' (ibid., p. 145).

6. Aped, Mongrelised and Scapegoated: Adventures in Biopolitics and Transgenics in Haraway's Animal Worlds

The domestic animal is the epoch-changing tool, realizing human intention in the flesh, in a dogsbody version of onanism. Man took the (free) wolf and made the (servant) dog and so made civilization possible. Mongrelized Hegel and Freud in the kennel?[1]

We saw in Chapter 3 some attempts, most notably by Jacques Derrida and by Deleuze and Guattari, to frame our concepts of animality in terms other than traditional taxonomy would allow, in particular against the grain of hierarchical classifications of animal life in which 'human' inevitably signifies 'superior'. In Deleuze and Guattari's works (specifically *A Thousand Plateaus* and *What is Philosophy?*) this alternative animality addresses certain lacunae in our thinking towards non-human species without necessarily making recourse to the moral assumption that we treat other animals cruelly or unjustly and that we must improve our treatment of them. Donna Haraway, not forgetting Deleuze and Guattari's belittlement of people who like cats and dogs (so-called Oedipal animals), pulls no punches in condemning their descriptions of 'becoming-other' (-woman, -child, -animal) as leaning towards 'misogyny, fear of aging, incuriosity about animals, and horror at the ordinariness of flesh, here covered by the alibi of an anti-Oedipal and anticapitalist project'.[2] Rethinking her deployment of the figure of the cyborg as an image useful for critical contemplation of the relations between living organisms and technology, and beyond the Deleuzian idea of becoming-animal, Haraway moves, as Braidotti comments, 'a step beyond the Oedipal configuration of the culture of familiar pets by proposing a new kinship system that includes "companion species" alongside other siblings and relatives'.[3] For Haraway, from her own experiences as a 'dog person' (never to be referred to as a 'dog *owner*'), productive reflections on the formation of relations between companion species can be gained from observing the range of human dealings with the domestic dog (a relationship that is also at the centre of Grandin's book, *Animals in Translation*, for its long history and potential to yield insights into the co-evolution of dogs and human beings). With the Deleuzian derogation of domestic canines in mind, perhaps, Haraway defends her choice of subject against the Western stereotypes of them as 'furry children'. Rather, dogs 'are not a projection, nor the realization of an intention, nor the *telos* of anything. They are dogs; i.e., a species in obligatory, constitutive, historical, protean relationship with human beings. The relationship is not especially nice; it is full of waste, cruelty, indifference, ignorance and loss, as well as joy, invention, labor, intelligence and play.'[4]

In *The Companion Species Manifesto*, Haraway also reflects further on the philosophical influences on her writing, in particular her affinity with the thought of Alfred North Whitehead in which its 'refusal of typological thinking, binary dualisms, and both relativisms and universalisms of many flavors, contributes a rich array of approaches to emergence, process, historicity, difference, specificity, co-habitation, co-constitution, and contingency'.[5] We saw how, in the philosophy of organism, it was not the already-constituted relations of subjects and objects that served as ultimate ground for experience, but rather the more microscopic sets of interrelations between 'actual occasions' that coalesced in different degrees of complexity and at different levels, such that our understanding of philosophically (and morally) relevant relations could be cut along multiple lines and levels. It is this malleability of the concept of relation that would allow us to think about the laboratory, the technician, and the rat as forming at once a perceptual, technical and cultural nexus. In Whitehead's sense, it is a collection of prehensions: in this case, the lab-rat-human 'subject', but also the transgenic OncoMouse (human-cancer-mouse), which I will discuss in the final section of this chapter. Haraway often deploys these conjunctions that echo Whitehead's openness to the formation of subjectivities from all of the elements that colour or influence what we normally think of as intersubjective relationships. Put simply, this helps to give expression to the way in which a human and a rat, for example, enter into a different kind of relationship when brought together in a laboratory rather than in a family home.

Alongside Whitehead (and in spite of Deleuze), Haraway's other favoured source is Derrida's writings, in which questions of moral responsibility undoubtedly underpin his insight that we have tended to overlook the significance of individual animal lives. It is *this* cat standing before me that deserves consideration, rather than *the animal*, which is a concept that can serve as trope, symbol, or mask for the *other* that is merely constitutive of the human self; and it is this relation of a single human being to the particular animal before her that is of sole importance in deciding how to treat that animal.[6] Each laboratory technician, each participant in a hunt, each marksman in a cull, each worker in an abattoir is implicated in a relationship of responsibility towards each individual animal before them, and the outcomes of such situations (the harms or deaths caused) ultimately belong to them, even if wider factors and conditions (cultural norms around the consumption of meat, the acceptance of animal experimentation as essential in medical research, and so on) have led them to that point.

Elisabeth de Fontenay underlines the significance of Derrida's stance in her short book, *Without Offending Humans* (originally published in French in 2008). In this text, she professes a certain affinity with Derrida's writings on animals, or the 'trace' of the animal question that persists throughout his works, noting that her own substantial piece of work on the history of philosophical engagements with animals, *Le silence des bêtes* (1999), was published in parallel with Derrida's conference paper that became the text, 'The Animal That Therefore I Am'.[7] To illustrate this common thread, de Fontenay identifies three levels of deconstruction that emerge from Derrida's work and that guide her own analyses of animal life. The first concerns a strategy '*through* the animal' in which the human/animal boundary has constantly been problematised in the history of philosophy:

> In the most recent version of this deconstruction of the man/animal division, one notes the determinate manner with which a generality, *the animal*, or, what comes down to more or less the same thing, of a tropological bestiary – animal figures – transforms into a multiplicity, *animals*, an immensely effective and effectuated multiplicity of *other* living beings that does not allow itself to be homogenized into the category of animal without violence or motivated ignorance.[8]

The second level concerns, as discussed earlier, a shift in consideration of a *singular* or *unique* animal: for example, the hedgehog in 'What is Poetry?' and the cat in 'The Animal That Therefore I Am'.[9] The latter text also gives rise, finally, to the third level of deconstruction which introduces the relation of *compassion* towards animals, and demands the reconfiguration, from the point of view of politics and ethics, of our obligations and responsibilities towards animals in the light of an acknowledgement of our violence towards them.[10] This elaboration of the animal question, from general taxonomy to issues of individual treatment and responsibility, is similarly taken up by Donna Haraway, again with an explicit indebtedness to Derrida for realising that 'actual animals look back at actual human beings'.[11] Haraway goes on to criticise Derrida for not thinking in enough detail about the cat as 'companion', and thus embarks on the task of elaborating what it means to relate to other animals as 'companion species'.

The first section of this chapter will focus on two chapters from Haraway's *Primate Visions*, on the construction of animals as scientific-technical objects (compare the interventions of scientific ideology, as outlined earlier in Chapter 4), and on a not entirely unproblematic examination of non-Western examples of scientific studies of animals (in countries such as Japan and India), in which the potential for thinking animals as companions emerges in Haraway's analysis of one Japanese scientist's idiosyncratic formulation of *kyokan* as a relation of 'shared life' established between scientific observer and observed animal, one that is intended to yield the most useful insights within the context of field studies of wild animals.

In her 2008 book, *When Species Meet*, in a chapter entitled, 'Sharing Suffering: Instrumental Relations between Laboratory Animals and Their People', Haraway seeks to address issues relating to the use of animals for research, including the infliction of pain and death in the course of this research. Haraway's chapter includes a survey of a range of positions held in the recent history of philosophy, from the traditional 'rights' discourse with its inheritance of early modern characterisations of subjective sovereignty, to twentieth-century engagements with the question such as Derrida's 'The Animal That Therefore I Am', which laments the inadequacy of discussions centred on the logic of sacrifice. Haraway's own position is characteristically eclectic, and in the second section of this chapter I will examine in more detail the stance she adopts based on the writings of Whitehead. The latter's professed interest in pre-Kantian philosophies (that is, philosophies *not* grounded on a unity of subjectivity) for the alternative articulation of terms such as 'relation' and 'subject' finds its echo in Haraway's resistance to describing the relations between animals and humans, or animals and other animals, in terms of subject/object dichotomies. I will examine how she proposes to rethink the lab-animal-human relation in other terms, such as labour/shared work, or in terms of shared suffering: what she terms 'nonmimetic suffering' in which the experimenter takes care to understand the suffering of the animal in order to understand how best to minimise their pain.

Despite this endeavour, and as I will argue in the final part of this chapter, Haraway herself raises a number of difficult questions, that confront her own work, concerning the sacrificial status of laboratory animals in an earlier essay entitled 'FemaleMan©_Meets_ OncoMouse™'. Haraway uses the figure of the OncoMouse to pose questions about its sacrificial status attained through the positioning of the lives of human beings suffering from certain diseases, in this case breast cancer, against the lives of 'lower' animals who serve as their 'scapegoat'. While the practices of shared suffering and a better understanding of cross-species communication (through either labour or play) could certainly help to improve our treatment of other animals, a persisting difficulty arises in the tendency – culturally or scientifically – to re-inscribe the hierarchy of human over animal, based on the calculation of value.

APES OF OUR IDEAL

Haraway's *Primate Visions*, in its historical study of the science of primatology, offers two alternative, and conflicting, perspectives on the impact of primate studies on human attitudes towards apes and monkeys. First, primates act as a 'distorted mirror image' of humanity, where it is more the case that human (cultural) assumptions about hierarchies of male/female and culture/nature are 'discovered' in rudimentary form in (that is, read into) primate behaviour, attesting to the influence of certain scientific ideologies particular to primatology. Haraway contends that primatological studies have essentially emerged as a kind of 'simian orientalism' (after Edward Said's text).[12] Just as 'the orient' has held, problematically, a certain place in Western history as the place of the origin of language and civilisation, as the West's 'Other', similarly, primate groups hold this place in relation to human societies as the 'cradle of culture'.[13] Thus Haraway's text poses questions about how the sciences have constructed primates as pre-figurations of the human, or simpler models of humanity whose behaviours can be manipulated in order to recreate the conditions of emergence of human social characteristics, and whose 'primitive' behaviours accentuate the process of evolutionary refinement that has taken place on the path towards *Homo sapiens*: 'Traditionally associated with lewd meanings, sexual lust, and the unrestrained body, monkeys and apes mirror humans in a complex play of distortions over centuries of western commentary on these troubling doubles.'[14]

Secondly, Haraway sees in primate studies a place to explore paths of resistance. Where previously (as we saw in Chapter 4) Haraway pointed to the potential for the dissolution of boundaries in the image of the cyborg, she shifts her focus here to animals as companion species. These are animals with whom we enter into what Deleuze and Guattari call 'unnatural participations': 'Primates existing at the boundaries of so many hopes and interests are wonderful subjects with whom to explore the permeability of walls, the reconstitution of boundaries, the distaste for endless socially enforced dualisms.'[15] Illustrations of this dual potentiality of the study of primate subjects can be found in Haraway's reflections on the experiments of Harry Harlow on rhesus monkeys that were designed to test the development and disorders of infant-parent relations. They can also be found in Haraway's attempts to resist a re-inscription of orientalism in her survey of scientific field study methodologies developed by scientists from non-Western countries, that might help to throw light upon Western methodologies, though not necessarily to supply 'better' or 'more authentic' alternatives.

In *Primate Visions*, Haraway goes on to analyse the personal motivations and broader social and cultural factors at play that influenced Harry Harlow's experiments, published from the 1960s onwards, in which infant rhesus monkeys were bred as 'tools' for a major programme of psychological experiments to compare human and simian rates and types of emotional development, most notably, the bond between infant and mother.[16] In order to test the development of this bond, the infant monkey was isolated from his natural mother and provided with a 'surrogate': usually comprised of a simple wire frame, covered in cloth, to which the infant monkey would instinctively cling. Variations of this cloth surrogate were constructed (with different coverings, with varying levels of 'hospitability': one particular surrogate emitted sharp spikes which would eject the infant monkey, in order to test whether the infant would return to his 'mother' despite 'her' apparent hostility). Haraway's analysis of this series of experiments raises a number of important problems concerning our wider attitudes towards the use of animals in scientific experiments. First of all, the problem discussed earlier in Chapter 2 of the 'ocularcentrism' and purism of the scientific gaze, is linked by Haraway to masculine power. For example, she contrasts the *National Geographic*'s favoured style of incorporating and foregrounding the relationship between the observer and the observed, with the absent figure of the scientist behind the cloth surrogate experiments, where 'neither nature nor author is represented in Harlow's iconography; only the inanimate surrogates and monkeys in their fully cultural form as experimental inhabitants of a laboratory colony are pictured in the scientific texts. The monkeys are even stripped of their "rhesus-specificity"; they are models and substitutes for human infants.'[17]

A second problem concerns the construction of the monkey as mirror of the human: it is a scientific-technical object, an indicator of human behaviour, but not itself a subject of suffering sufficient to prohibit its production in the first place. In the effort to reconstitute the rudiments of human emotional attachment in the rhesus monkey infants, the actual suffering of the monkeys – the reactions of fear, distress and retreat into the comfort of the mock-maternal embrace – is disregarded in favour of the analogue of human love that it offers up. The absence of the experimenter from both the images of the experimental scenarios and from any kind of direct relation with the monkey-subjects, effectively dissociating the human agent from responsibility for the induced emotional states of the monkey, starkly demonstrates the asymmetry of the human-animal relation in the context of the laboratory. It is this asymmetry that will pose particular, and perhaps insoluble, difficulties for Haraway's appeal to nonmimetic sharing that I will discuss in the next section of this chapter. A further problem arises in how we measure the value and contributions of such research to later understanding of human and animal behaviour, not through the constructed mirror image of the human, but perhaps, in the end, from problematisations of the human/animal boundary. While Haraway underlines the 'unintended irony' of these experiments that aimed to uncover the basic nature of maternal love as '*touch*, the bridging of distance ... the sensuous clinging of the nearly totally isolated monkey to the remnant of social life present in the cage, the cloth-covered surrogate',[18] Temple Grandin credits the experiments with revealing the effects of sensory deprivation on the development of a child's stable emotional state; in humans who suffer from sensory-processing disorders, normal emotional development is interrupted or inhibited.[19]

Harlow's experiments, characterised by confinement of the subjects to the laboratory, the panoptic gaze of the scientist, and the rendering of animality as distorting mirror of humanity, present us with the uglier aspects of the science of primatology. However, some contrasts drawn with methodological variants developed in 'non-Western' countries seem to offer potential for rethinking the human/animal boundary. Appealing to 'the East' of course carries the risk of committing the fallacy of orientalism (if one might refer to it as such), and Haraway herself cautions against this, observing that the east-west contrast would serve merely to highlight different scientific ideologies at work beneath the apparently neutral scientific methodologies, regardless of the nation in question. One significant feature she notes is that in opposition to the institution of boundaries (human/animal, mind/body) that seems to be characteristic of sciences born of Western philosophy and Judeo-Christian thought, methodologies arising from cultures with Buddhist and Confucian roots (such as Japan) seem to privilege status, personality and social change, where 'the split between observer and observed, so crucial to the western quest for a healing touch across the breach, is missing'.[20]

Several traits of Japanese primatology that Haraway identifies at least indicate a number of alternative scientific ideals of human-animal interaction and the absence of the idealised 'breach'. These include the practice of 'provisioning', or the feeding of animals in order to study them, which clashes with Western ideals of pure observation (either in controlled laboratory spaces or as a hidden observer in the field); she notes that feeding wild animals is seen as 'normal' in Japanese interactions with wildlife. Another observed trait is the recognition of individual animals by personality within their wider social order: 'The social conventions of the monkeys were precisely the natural-technical object of knowledge constructed by the Japanese observers.'[21] This opposes the 'Western' use of tags or abstract markers based on physical traits. Finally, what is effectively a synthesis of the other traits, is the coining by one scientist, Kawai Masao, of the term *kyokan* to signify the human observer's fusing with the observed animals in a 'shared life'. Such fusion is, furthermore, promoted '*as the basis for reliable scientific knowledge*'.[22] This is not equivalent to a Western concept of a 'romanticised organicism' that excludes power and violence. Rather, it entails participation in the existing social hierarchies of the animal group in question (which can include violence or aggression towards lower status members of the social group, for example). That Haraway places special emphasis on this term, *kyokan*, an idiosyncrasy of Kawai Masao rather than a reflection of Japanese observers as a whole, helps her to avoid the charge of appealing to the East to solve the problems of the West.

In Chapter 3 we saw how ascriptions of pathological status to certain animals, rather than levelling the biopolitical field, served to draw ever-renewing lines marking human versus non-human conflicts, and justifications for defence against threatening species (e.g. the grey squirrel or the ruddy duck, both 'invasive' migrants from North America to the UK). The example of India's prior resistance to the USA's demands for primate exports, and how it then enacted its own decimation of indigenous primate populations in the interests of economic growth through agricultural development, is another example of cross-cutting forces that have shaped attitudes towards animal life.[23] In her observations of the influence of Indian cultures on such attitudes, Haraway points out that the 'sacred' status granted to an animal does not equate to 'wildness', citing Indian culture as one in which interaction with wild monkeys is commonplace. Despite how it sounds, I would venture that this is not simply a primitivist idealisation of Eastern cultures in which the indigenous populations are somehow closer to nature and are thus able to interact more authentically with wild animals. One need only look, in the UK, at the interactions between human urban populations and species such as the squirrel, or indigenous and migratory bird populations. As we saw earlier, this is equally complicated in regard to species such as foxes, badgers and predatory birds (on certain estates raising wildfowl for hunting). These species have a more ambivalent status in UK discourses on wildlife conservation and 'management', and currently hover on the borderline between 'protected species' and 'pest', while pigeons (or, technically, rock doves) have the unenviable triple status of pet, pest and food source.

In the next section, we will see a return to these subtle differences in models of human-animal interaction in relation to the idea of nonmimetic sharing, not only in the promotion of the value of interacting with animals *on their own terms*, but also in the acceptance or acknowledgement of violence and power in these relations.

RETHINKING RELATION

The relation between human and non-human animals renegotiated as that between *companion species* develops the concept of *kyokan* discussed above in a number of ways. It resists Western metaphysical ideals of separation according to differences of kind where, for example, the mind/body distinction reinforces in turn dichotomies such as human rationality versus animal instinct. It also resists thinking in terms of differences of degree where non-human animals, particularly primates, tend to be seen as evolutionary precursors of human beings, reinforcing the basic human/animal distinction. As Birke and Parisi observe:

> This tendency to distance ourselves from a generic animal is one instance of . . . the 'homogenization of the colonized', in which the colonized Other is always seen in ways that reduce individuality. They are faceless Others. To contrast human with animal is thus to invoke a contrast with a mythical beast. Homogenization is common in racist and sexist rhetoric; but it applies also to how we conceptualize animals. To which ones are we claiming to be superior? And in which behavior or capability?[24]

Instead, thinking in terms of companion species favours thinking the relationships that exist now and that continue to be forged between humans and non-humans. Neither humanist nor posthumanist, it is a 'a not-humanism in which species of all sorts are in question'.[25] The relations that humans enter into with other animals are not simply unidirectional: other animals regard us as much as we regard them (the simple observation about Derrida's cat). Following Whitehead, Haraway promotes the idea of companion species as a 'permanently undesirable category ... that insists on the relation as the smallest unit of being and analysis'.[26] Examples of such relations include the lab-animal-human relation: here, all of the elements are connected by hyphens to indicate that the laboratory introduces particular conditions that colour the relationship between the human scientist and the animal 'test-subject'. Cut along different lines, Haraway cites the relationships between humans and dogs, in the worlds of dog breeding (of pure-breds), of clinical trials for veterinary medicines, and, in a reflection on her relationship with her own dog, the world of dog agility sports. All of these provide places to question and reconfigure the ways in which we view animals as companions, newly acknowledged subjects or others whose identities are fragmented and reconstituted continually, as groupings of prehensions are in the ever-renewing constitution of 'societies' at multiple levels of process.

If we follow Haraway's speculations, thinking about inter-species relationality in these terms places us on the path towards an ethics of flourishing and well-being, rather than one based on the alleviation of suffering. Citing bioethics as 'perhaps one of the most boring discourses to cross one's path in technoculture',[27] Haraway admonishes this field of ethical argument for its focus on regulation and prohibitions 'after the fact'; all of the interesting work takes place in the laboratory, work that in itself constitutes the exploration and 'ontological reshaping' of organic life. In the meantime, ethics plays 'catch-up with odd abstractions and bio-think-tank scenarios'.[28] The example that Haraway uses here is of the overlapping of science and flourishing in the practices of dog breeders, which aim to deal with the transmission of genetic canine disorders. Haraway acknowledges that pure-bred dogs are seen as products of human mastery and manipulation, as 'an affectation, an abuse, an abomination, the embodiment of animalising racist eugenics',[29] but argues, in the spirit of Derrida's exhortation to treat each animal as *someone* worthy of consideration, that these animals cannot be excluded from consideration just because they are products of artificial selection. The preservation and flourishing of species cannot simply be reserved for the privileged wild and endangered species such as the tiger, the panda and the orangutan, or indeed Deleuze and Guattari's noble savage of the (non-human) animal kingdom, the wolf.

a) Ethics as Cross-Species Communication

An ethics of flourishing is not, of course, novel, and other recent proponents of improved human-animal interactions based on 'cross-species' communication include feminist care ethicists such as Josephine

Donovan. Feminist animal care theory can be summed up as a reaction to the animal rights/utilitarian theories characterised by Singer and Regan, which privilege reason and mathematical calculation: 'Both rights and utilitarianism dispense with sympathy, empathy and compassion as relevant ethical and epistemological sources for human treatment of nonhuman animals.'[30] Donovan's alternative position is that 'We should not kill, eat, torture, and exploit animals because they do not want to be so treated, and we know that.'[31] Could we not, asks Donovan, extend feminist standpoint theory to animals, including their standpoint in our ethical deliberations?[32] In this scheme: 'humans pay attention to – listen to – animal communications and construct a human ethic in conversation with the animals rather than imposing on them a rationalistic, calculative grid of humans' own monological construction'.[33] That is, we should take into account animals' needs and wants by learning their ways of communicating. Despite the examples of Wittgenstein's lion (whose language we could not understand) and Nagel's bat (whose experience we could not comprehend), this is something that is in fact accessible to us as we tend to 'tune into' other forms of communication by observing non-verbal signs of pleasure and pain. Donovan argues that we should, furthermore, appreciate that empathy and sympathy do not, by themselves, ensure ethical behaviour in any situation. Therefore, the political situation in which the harm is perpetrated should also be taken into account: 'getting people to see evil and to care about suffering is a matter of clearing away ideological rationalisations that legitimate animal exploitation and cruelty. Recognising the egregious use of euphemism employed to disguise such behaviour . . . would seem to be an important step in this direction'.[34]

Along these lines a summary of the possibilities for non-patriarchal responses to animal ethical theorists such as Singer and Regan, principally against their derision of emotional and empathic responses to animal suffering, is provided in Brian Luke's essay, 'Taming Ourselves or Going Feral', in which he defines 'a *patriarchal* meta-ethics in relation to animal liberation' as a 'tacit acceptance of sexist derogations of female animal liberationists as overly sentimental or hysterical, leading to a distrust of emotion and an overemphasis on cold reason as the source of animal liberationism'.[35] On the other hand, it would be the goal of 'animal liberationist ethics' to uncover the conditions that ground our 'putatively uncaring dispositions toward animals', these conditions being the rational principles that serve as foundation for the closed circle of moral consideration. Tom Regan exemplifies the targeted patriarchal position when he argues for a rational, unemotional rethinking of the rights of other animals: 'We cannot justify harming [animals] merely on the grounds that this will produce an optimal aggregate balance of intrinsic goods over intrinsic evils for all concerned. We owe them respectful treatment, not out of kindness, nor because of the "sentimental interests" of others, but because justice requires it.'[36] In response to such a position, Luke sets out some of the key characteristics of this form of patriarchal meta-ethics, and suggests some ways of remedying the effects of these characteristics in non-patriarchal ways. In the case of pejorative references to emotion, by which both Singer and Regan attempt to 'rescue' animal liberationist ethics from its association with mere sentiment, Luke argues that such a reaction simply participates in a *gendered* attitude to emotion that can be counteracted by uncovering and dismantling the underlying sexism:

> A central patriarchal ideology is the elevation of the 'rational/cultural' male over the 'emotional/biological' female. Women's rage (labelled 'sentiment', 'hysteria', etc.) is thus divested of political significance by interpreting any female reaction against the established order not as a moral challenge to that order, but as a bio[logical]-sexual phenomenon to be ignored or subdued.[37]

In order to overcome one's immediate emotional responses, a set of abstract first principles is used to underpin rules of conduct, which thereby bring those emotional responses under control. And so, Luke continues, theorists such as Singer and Regan conclude their studies with a set of guiding principles to which we, once we have 'seen reason', can adhere, such as advocating universal vegetarianism or a 'qualified anti-vivisectionism'.[38] For de Fontenay and Haraway, like Derrida, the alternative is to reconsider our own agency and that of other animals within the network of relations that we, as individuals, form with one another.

Luke continues with an analysis of the ways in which animal ethics and our wider attitudes towards other animals can be described in one of two senses: (i) under the banner of 'taming ourselves' and (ii) under that of 'going feral'. The way in which animal ethical theorists such as Singer and Regan portray emotion as something inconsistent or undependable seems to be mirrored in the very industries that they seek to criticise. For example, the human feelings of repulsion at animal harm and cruelty are, in fact, *so* reliable that 'every institution of animal exploitation develops some means of undercutting them'.[39] Anecdotes from slaughterhouses, animal laboratories, and so on, illustrate the way in which individuals who first come to work in such places have to undergo a process of distancing themselves from the animals they are working on. The animals must be seen no longer as sentient, feeling beings, but as instruments, or cases, or even isolated body parts, all in the effort to divest them of any subjectivity. It would, then, seem counter to an animal liberationist ethics (in Singer's sense) that it should have at its centre the project of distancing itself from emotional reactions to animal suffering, in favour of a presupposed universal rational sense of moral behaviour. Both the animal industries and the ethical frameworks that seek to control them are underpinned by a need or a drive to 'tame ourselves', to bring emotional responses under control; whereas, in the promotion of 'going feral' the project of animal liberation:

> is not furthered by imposing controls (reason over natural indifference), but by *breaking through* the controls on animal-human connection to which we are subject. Since those controls are limitations on our integrated agency, animal liberation can be seen, metaethically, as a process of human moral development, an extension (often a reclamation) of our capacities as agents.[40]

In the light of these two examples of reconfigured human-animal ethical relations, we will see how Haraway responds to the problems of both cross-species communication and the centrality of empathy and emotion, in order to provide alternative foundations for ethical relations.

Following Donovan's emphasis on enhancing human-animal communication, Haraway discusses the forms of communication that exist, often unacknowledged, not just between humans and non-humans but also across species boundaries amongst non-human animals. She cites examples of relationships of 'play' developed between domestic animals (a dog and a donkey no less; but perhaps also Haraway's own relationship with her dog, 'Cayenne Pepper', anecdotes about which are interlaced throughout *When Species Meet*) in which it seems that there is some exploitation of the predator-prey dynamic that would otherwise exist between a carnivore and a herbivore. Such a relationship has, it seems, been built upon an evolved mutual understanding, and the dis-aggregation and reconstitution of the predator-prey dynamics in *play* that does not simply function here as a rehearsal for future behaviour (the common interpretation of play in young animals), but is rather an exercise of *joy* (purposeless activity that is not linked to *desire*).[41] To defend this line of thinking as more than an anthropomorphic ascription of linguistic ability to non-humans, Haraway notes that even prominent linguists (such as Noam Chomsky) acknowledge that the burden of proof now lies with those who hold on to the exclusivity of language to human beings; we have to prove that the complex of behaviours and processes of forming both intra- and inter-species relations and responses amongst animals are *not* linguistic in nature.[42] Like Josephine Donovan, Haraway promotes the learning of animals' own means of communication, and 'the corporeal semiosis of cross-species trust',[43] in order to better understand the conditions of their flourishing.

(b) Nonmimetic Suffering

The second type of relation, emotional and empathic, is discussed by Haraway in terms of the practice of sharing suffering, which she hopes can be promoted amongst scientists as a means of improving understanding of the needs of animals kept in laboratories. Her chosen example is that of a Zimbabwean man (referred to as Baba Joseph) who experiments on guinea pigs to test the effects of certain poisons on biting flies. The guinea pigs are placed into a small wire cage so that they are unable to move while being subjected to the flies' bites. For Haraway the important feature of this experiment is that the man also puts his own arm into the cage in order to feel and understand what the rodents are experiencing, to share their suffering 'nonmimetically', the meaning of which is explained in the following way: '[Baba Joseph] sustained bites not to stand in as experimental object but to understand the rodents' suffering so as to do what he could about it, even if that was only to serve as witness to the need for something properly called forgiveness even in the most thoroughly justified instances of causing suffering.'[44]

Haraway does not call for an end to experimentation on animals, but rather for an acknowledgement that animals 'have a face' (in spite of Levinas' doubts), and that this demands 'recognition, caring, and shared pain'.[45] This recognition of, and responsibility for, the suffering of laboratory animals should form the basis for changes in practices that make the laboratory 'less deadly, less painful, and freer' for all concerned: 'The problem is to learn to live responsibly within the multiplicitous necessity and labor of killing, so as to be in the open, in quest of the capacity to respond in relentless historical, nonteleological, multispecies contingency.'[46]

If this seems insufficient, Haraway herself recognises that it would fall short as an answer for most animal advocates (animal rights activists). She highlights the difficulties with the idea of sharing suffering which operates with reference firstly to her recourse to Whitehead on the fragmentation and ever-renewing reconstitution of trans-individual relations which allows us to think conjunctions of human-machine, human-animal, animal-machine as subjects deserving of consideration (framed in the terms of Stengers' cosmopolitical relations).[47] Secondly, in her recourse to Derrida to acknowledge the lives of individual animals for which we are responsible, or whose lives are 'response-able' (that is, capable of provoking a response), none of this yet answers the question about which particular practices are actually to be advocated in laboratories that would make the lives of each animal significantly better. Haraway's answer remains speculative with regard to vertebrate animals (e.g. paying for the recruitment and training of staff responsible for the 'enrichment' of the animals' environments, requiring such staff as necessary members of any laboratory team, in much the same way as is promoted in other captive animal environments such as zoos). She concludes with examples garnered from colleagues who work predominantly with invertebrate animals or who limit themselves to the use of 'subjects' such as reptile eggs.[48] While important, this defers the question and uncovers little evidence amongst the scientific community that the practice of nonmimetic sharing as opening to the human-lab-animal relationship is being taken up where it matters: in the large, well-funded laboratories engaged in medical and pharmaceutical research on predominantly vertebrate animals.

Another alternative model for the role of animals in the laboratory is provided by Haraway in her re-thinking of animals as 'labourers', appealing to the example of research on dogs suffering from haemophilia. In this context, the dogs are treated first and foremost as patients requiring care for their haemophilia and, second, as patients in clinical trials. Haraway suggests that the displacement of 'research animals' from laboratories to homes in care of their 'owners' (animal owners or handlers taking on the role of 'caregivers') is at least preferable to the industrial-scale breeding of animals, in particular those bred specifically to develop pathological conditions for the purposes of research.[49]

There is a tension here between Haraway's concerns about the care of terminally ill patients (human and non-human) and her hesitation to come out in opposition to animal experimentation. On the one hand, she is concerned about the questionable wisdom of subjecting dogs to prolonged treatment for terminal conditions such as cancer (with chemotherapy and experimental therapies), paralleling the issues arising from the participation of human subjects in similar trials, in which they often endure painful treatments in the name of the search for cures. In such endeavours we have risked losing sight of the natural termination of life, or the internal nature of processes of disease and death (thereby giving rise to the contentious debates over euthanasia and whether killing can ever be a kindness).[50] On the other hand, as we will see in Haraway's use of the example of the OncoMouse and other laboratory animals, such instances are not necessarily condemned but are rather presented as cases in which killing can be justified on the basis that their sacrifice can help cancer sufferers who, it seems, must be saved at all costs.

This tension is also famously played out, as Haraway notes, in the novels of J. M. Coetzee. The hard-line animal rights position on the meat industry, where meat is murder, and the meat industry is comparable to the Holocaust, as in Coetzee's *Lives of Animals*, signals an absolute inability to tolerate animal death; whereas the problem of justified killing in Coetzee's novel *Disgrace*, by contrast, arises in the story of a veterinarian compelled to deal with the problem of abandoned dogs and cats through mass euthanasia. Is killing on a massive scale for food comparable to killing abandoned (and one presumes unsaveable) animals, other than in terms of a calculation? The familiar appeal to compassion to argue that both forms of killing are wrong or undesirable, from the point of view of the animal rights advocate, operates relatively unproblematically. However, Haraway's questioning, at this point, seems merely to reiterate the dilemma before us regarding the limited terms of traditional moral philosophy and Derrida's retort to it: individual, historically located, animal lives are forgotten under the terms of reasoned moral argument. Coetzee's two novels play out the tension between unjust and just killing, but the question about whether impending 'natural death' in humans (suffering from terminal conditions) removes some of the justifications for vivisection remains. For example, medical conditions that arise from the natural process of ageing, such as cancer and dementia, form an ever-receding boundary between what counts as 'normal' and 'pathological' in humans.

The need to search for cures for such conditions, highlighted by medical professionals as the highest causes of mortality amongst varying groups of the population, is presented as a justification for research on animals, while the prevalence of such diseases associated with ageing continues to rise with the introduction of more efficient systems of public healthcare and screening programmes that contribute to the prolongation of human life.

ONCOMOUSE

Consider the contrasting fates of a cat and a mouse, both, as it happens, under Canadian law: the first in the context of criminal proceedings, and the second in the deliberations of the Canadian Patent Office.

In 2002, a domestic cat (nicknamed 'Kensington') from a Toronto suburb was caught and, in front of a video camera, mutilated while still conscious, and finally killed. The video, lasting seventeen minutes, became the key evidence in a criminal case brought against the perpetrator and two accomplices. The prosecutors pressed a charge of 'mischief' (against property) against the perpetrators, as well as one of animal cruelty, on the basis that the former charge carried with it a more severe penalty (mischief carrying a two-year imprisonment penalty; while animal cruelty carried a lesser punishment of imprisonment for up to six months and a $2000 fine).[51] Lesli Bisgould notes the problematic duality in the status of domestic animals under Canadian law specifically, but with implications for considerations of the status of animals under law internationally. Haraway also underlines this link between domestication and the exercise of power over animals denied the status of subjects where, even grammatically, they are not allowed the personal pronouns of *he*, *she*, or *who*, and instead are correctly referred to as *that*, *it* or *which* (and I have tended to follow Haraway, here, in my use of personal pronouns whenever I have referred to animals in the course of this book, however ungrammatical that may be).[52]

The second case concerns the OncoMouse, a genetically engineered 'transgenic' mouse that was designed by Harvard University scientists to develop a form of human breast cancer for the purposes of research into the progress of the disease.[53] Due to the novelty of its transgenic status, the OncoMouse became the first animal to be subject to patent laws in the United States. The patent was subsequently granted in Europe, but rejected in Canada. Rosemary Robins argues that the differing outcomes of the patent applications in the USA, Europe and Canada were the result of their arrivals at different levels of 'coherence', a legal term used to describe:

> an understanding of how objects can be simultaneously singular and multiple. The singularity of an object, in this case the oncomouse as patentable invention, is contingent upon multiple enactments of that object, in this case as natural animal, research tool and invention, that intersect, overlap and depend upon one another – that cohere. Law describes this way of writing about objects as a 'fractional knowing' that does not efface the object's multiplicity.[54]

The Canadian Patent Office received protests against the patent by animal advocate, environmental and other lobby groups, such as Compassion in World Farming and the British Union for the Abolition of Vivisection, who argued under the terms of the calculation of relative benefits that 'the oncomouse was of limited usefulness when it came to testing such things as anti-cancer drugs, and non-animal alternatives were available'.[55] But the office itself was focused on establishing the characteristic of the animal that could qualify as the product of human invention (the 'composition of matter' that could be patented). It ruled that the product of invention was restricted to gene manipulations that were completed outside the body of the mouse, while the mouse itself was gestated *in utero* and was thus the product of nature which was not patentable.[56]

In the one case, the cat needed to be reduced in the terms of the law to the status of property in order for the penalty to entail some recognition, if indirectly, of his suffering. In the other case, the mouse's life could not be reduced adequately enough to the status of property, in terms of the patent office's definition of a 'composition of matter', for the application of a patent to be granted. Such has been the contradictory status of domestic animals under the eyes of the law.

Haraway's own thoughts on the OncoMouse, in her essay 'FemaleMan©_Meets_OncoMouse™', are, primarily, inflected with her reading of Foucauldian biopolitics. From this perspective, she is principally concerned with the figure of the transgenic organism as a means of thinking about the implications and interactions between science, technology, biotechnology and global capitalism, amongst other forces, and repeating her ambitions for the figures of the cyborg and companion species as tools of critique. In view of the implications of Haraway's later text, *When Species Meet* (as I discussed in the last section) in which the well-being of individual animals, including, and perhaps especially, laboratory animals, becomes of paramount importance, we can ask whether transgenic organisms, whose existence for Haraway is so intimately bound up with debates about the transgressing of borders, racial purity, and natural kinds, are precluded from consideration as individuals and therefore as capable of flourishing.

The mobile category of the pathological expresses the uncertain or double status as promise of a cure (scapegoat) and threat of contamination (genetic anomaly) of such organisms whose transsubjectivity has been determined at a genetic level. What possibilities, beyond nonmimetically shared suffering, lie in the lives of these organisms? First of all, the OncoMouse blurs the boundaries between technology and politics, nature and society, in Haraway's project to 'help put the boundary between the technical and the political back into permanent question as part of the obligation of building situated knowledges inside the materialised narrative fields of technoscience'.[57] That is, one key aim is to build, or restore, situated knowledges, or acknowledge the inherent perspectivism of scientific discourses. As we saw in Canguilhem, and as Haraway's studies of primatology demonstrated, the life sciences have proceeded, in an apparently objectivist manner, with a tendency to hide or deny the reality of their unconscious metaphysics or cultural biases.

Canguilhem and Haraway have shown us that biological research has tended to be both ideologically invested and to serve as a space for the blurring of boundaries. Returning also to Bergson, for us to understand living processes, that is, the conditions of our own emergence and continued existence, we must turn scrutiny back upon our own modes of thought. We are not indifferent observers of life; we *are* life, and we constantly risk losing sight of our own implication in living processes. As Haraway demonstrates, we need to rethink our relation to other living things in the new world of biotechnological experimentation and informatics, in terms of the networks of relations that we constitute and reconstitute along ever-renewing lines in response to advancements in technology, our understanding of biological processes, and our interfaces with both technology and biology that reshape one another along the way.

To underscore the significance of the production of transgenic animals for our thinking of the relations between humans, non-humans and technology, not just as a playful reconfiguration of relation (as one might characterise artistic adventures in 'becoming-animal'), but rather as a vital reconfiguration, Haraway draws a comparison between 'transuranic' elements and transgenic organisms. Recounting the history of the manufacture of plutonium (with an atomic number, or 'weight', of 94 on the periodic scale), derived from the naturally occurring uranium (atomic number 92), thus making it a 'transuranic' element, Haraway emphasises how plutonium, in its apparently simple manufactured difference, has come to fuel nuclear reactors and weapons, while its manufacture, as well as the post-Cold War illegal trade in it from the former Soviet Union, and the global amassing of a material that cannot be disposed of, has changed the landscape of human existence. Transuranic elements thus have two key features:

> First, they are ordinary, natural offspring of the experimental way of life, whose place in the periodic table was ready for them. They fit right in. Second, they are earthshaking artificial productions of technoscience whose status as aliens on earth, and indeed in the entire solar system, has changed who we are fundamentally and permanently.[58]

The enormous impact that this technological development has had on our thinking of global human relations is mirrored in the development of transgenic organisms. Non-human animals spliced with human DNA do not 'fit into well-established taxonomic and evolutionary discourses and also blast widely understood senses of natural limit'.[59] The uncertain status of transgenic animals not only highlights the shifting grounds of biological classification and of the conflicting terms of ownership and guardianship under which animals can variously be considered under the law, it also exposes the limited terms with which animal activists tend to operate in protesting against the practice of animal experimentation. To defend the lives of animals against their reduction to research tools, recourse is often made to 'the integrity of natural kinds and the natural *telos* or self-defining purpose of all life forms'.[60] Furthermore, Haraway regrets the reduction and simplification of scientific discourses, in the name of animal advocacy, that only serve to polarise through distortion the potential debates over the use of animals for research. For example: 'this appeal to sustain other organisms' inviolable, intrinsic natures is intended to affirm their difference from humanity and their claim on lives lived on their terms and not "man's" ... is a problematic argument resting on unconvincing biology'.[61] At worst, such arguments for genetic integrity and purism convey 'the unintended tones of fear of the alien and suspicion of the mixed'.[62]

However, in the case of wild animals, is it simply purist to argue that confinement of animals to cages (in laboratories, zoos, circuses) for much of their lives is detrimental to their well-being, in the sense that the inability to express natural behaviours increases the risk and incidence of physical and psychological disease? To answer such a question, and without appealing to established taxonomical boundaries and received notions of what counts as natural, Haraway calls for serious debate and productive engagements between all the interested groups, and names the laboratory as the significant site in which these debates can take place, because 'the laboratory is an arrangement and concentration of human and nonhuman actors, action, and results that change entities, meanings, and lives on a global scale'.[63] The critical significance of the laboratory, reflecting at once the speed and gravity of the boundary redefinitions that modern bio-scientific research is capable of inducing, is, then, made manifest in the figure of the OncoMouse. This creature's very existence poses difficult questions, as much for animal advocates as for scientific researchers:

> Although her promise is decidedly secular, she is a figure in the sense developed within Christian realism: S/he is our scapegoat; s/he bears our suffering; s/he signifies and enacts our mortality in a powerful, historically specific way that promises a culturally privileged kind of salvation – 'a cure for cancer.' Whether I agree to her existence and use or not, s/he suffers, physically, repeatedly, and profoundly, that I and my sisters may live.[64]

The figure of the scapegoat captures the sense of the OncoMouse as bearer of the 'sins' (as suffering, vulnerability and susceptibility to disease) of humanity and its status as 'outcast', belonging neither to animal nor human kinds. However, it exists perhaps more poignantly as a recurring symbol of condoned animal sacrifice. From the biblical story of Abraham and Isaac to Kierkegaard's *Fear and Trembling*, and in the re-enactment of this story today in rituals of animal slaughter performed by certain religious groups, the notion of sacrifice is significant for the act of faith entailed, but never for the death of the animal. The image of the scapegoat/sacrifice signifying the subjection of animals to often cruel treatment in order to benefit human life, also signifies that such benevolence to humans must simultaneously recognise the animals' own susceptibility to suffering and disease. Without such susceptibility, animals could not serve as adequate substitutes for humans in medical research. In this sense, the scapegoat is not so much a justification for killing, but instead provides the perfect articulation of the problematic duality of human-animal interactions.

Ultimately, in cases of animals such as the OncoMouse, Haraway states her opposition to moves such as the patenting of living organisms, not only as a move that itself commits the fallacy of biological reductionism (organisms are reducible to their genome, and thus human manipulations of genes are sufficient to qualify as 'inventions'). She also notes that:

> Because patent status reconfigured an organism as a human invention, produced by mixing labor and nature as those categories are understood in Western law and philosophy, patenting an organism is a large semiotic and practical step toward blocking nonproprietary and nontechnical meaning from many social sites – such as labs, courts and popular venues.[65]

That is, patenting carries with it the potential to preclude serious debate about the treatment of laboratory and other domestic and captive animals, when they are reduced to the status of property and technical objects. We have, however, also seen that the fates of other animal lives, even considered in the apparently benevolent terms of stewardship or guardianship of nature, remain equally uncertain. In recent debates about 'culling' of badgers, deer and other wild animals, appeal is made to the need to curb the animals' population growth, in order to avoid stresses on their habitats, which would otherwise result in excessive competition for resources. The option of culling, it is argued, is seen to benefit the future health and well-being of the animal population as a whole.

In summary, the existence of transgenic animals implies several interacting, and sometimes conflicting, conclusions about the concepts of life and animality under the gaze of the contemporary life sciences. On the one hand, animals bred specifically to develop pathological conditions, such as the OncoMouse, bear within them some of the particular 'hallmarks' of pathological life and 'non-life'. That is, as syntheses of human DNA (in pathological mode) and animal hosts, they are a threat to the integrity of the gene pools of natural populations of both mammalian species. Their existence begs the question: If there is an argument for allowing a 'natural death' for human cancer sufferers (and sufferers of other terminal diseases), can we not extend this to include animal cancer sufferers, such as the 'Oncomice', and prohibit their breeding and use for research? On the other hand, transgenic animals are also, at one and the same time, the property of humans, the products of technology, technical objects and natural living organisms (in legal terms, they 'cohere'). Thinking life, at its core, as pathological, has led to a blurring of the boundary between nature and technics. We have seen the shift from thinking pathology as natural and internal to organic bodies, to its status as the product of invention and as a technical object in the service of research. It is across all examples of human interventions in animal existence, in domestication, in the captivity of wild animals, and in transgenics, that the devitalisation of life occurs, and it is in this 'crucible' of the natural, technical, political and ethical that debates about our treatment of our animal others must commence.

NOTES

1. Donna Haraway, *The Companion Species Manifesto* (Chicago: Prickly Paradigm Press, 2003), pp. 27–8.
2. Donna Haraway, *When Species Meet* (Minneapolis: University of Minnesota Press, 2008), p. 30.
3. Braidotti, 'Posthuman, All Too Human', p. 203.
4. Haraway, *The Companion Species Manifesto*, pp. 11–12.
5. Ibid., pp. 6–7.
6. Cf. Giorgio Agamben, *The Open* (Stanford: Stanford University Press, 2004), on the reduction of the animal to the sacrificial element necessary for the constitution of human identity by means of the 'anthropological machine'.
7. Elisabeth de Fontenay, *Without Offending Humans: A Critique of Animal Rights* (Minneapolis: Minnesota University Press, 2012), p. 2.
8. Ibid., p. 3.
9. Ibid., pp. 4–7.
10. Ibid., p. 8.
11. Haraway, *When Species Meet*, p. 19.
12. See Edward Said, *Orientalism* (London: Penguin, 2003).
13. Donna Haraway, *Primate Visions: Gender, Race, and Nature in the World of Modern Science* (New York: Routledge, 1989).
14. Haraway, *Primate Visions*, p. 11.
15. Ibid., p. 3.

16. See, for example, Harry Harlow, 'The Nature of Love', *American Psychologist*, 13, 1958.
17. Haraway, *Primate Visions*, p. 234.
18. Ibid.
19. See Chapter 3 above and Temple Grandin's *Thinking in Pictures*.
20. Haraway, *Primate Visions*, p. 246.
21. Ibid., p. 251.
22. Ibid., p. 252.
23. Ibid., p. 263.
24. Lynda Birke and Luciana Parisi, 'Animals, Becoming', in H. Peter Steeves (ed.), *Animal Others* (New York: SUNY Press, 1999), pp. 59–60.
25. Haraway, *When Species Meet*, p. 164.
26. Ibid., p. 165.
27. Ibid., p. 136.
28. Ibid., p. 137.
29. Ibid., p. 96.
30. Josephine Donovan, 'Feminism and the Treatment of Animals: From Care to Dialogue', in S. J. Armstrong and R. G. Botzler (eds), *The Animal Ethics Reader*, 2nd edn (London: Routledge, 2003), p. 48.
31. Ibid., p. 47.
32. Ibid.
33. Ibid., p. 48.
34. Ibid., p. 51.
35. Brian Luke, 'Taming Ourselves or Going Feral', in Carol Adams and Josephine Donovan (eds), *Animals and Women: Feminist Theoretical Perspectives* (Durham, NC: Duke University Press, 1995), p. 291.
36. Regan, *The Case for Animal Rights*, p. 261.
37. Luke, 'Taming Ourselves or Going Feral', p. 293.
38. Ibid., p. 295.
39. Ibid., p. 312.
40. Ibid., p. 313.
41. Haraway, *When Species Meet*, pp. 232–4.
42. Ibid., p. 237.
43. Ibid., p. 243.
44. Ibid., p. 75.
45. Ibid., p. 71.
46. Ibid., p. 80.
47. Cf. Isabelle Stengers, *Cosmopolitics I* (Minneapolis: University of Minnesota Press, 2010).
48. Haraway, *When Species Meet*, p. 86.
49. Ibid., p. 58 ff.
50. Haraway makes reference here to Foucault's study of the birth of the clinic, as a way of thinking about the conjunction of movements across medicine, public health, the pet industry and agribusiness (Haraway, *When Species Meet*, p. 64).

51. Lesli Bisgould, 'Power and Irony: One Tortured Cat and Many Twisted Angles to Our Moral Schizophrenia About Animals', in Jodey Castricano (ed.), *Animal Subjects: An Ethical Reader in a Posthuman World* (Waterloo: Wilfrid Laurier University Press, 2008), p. 260.

52. Haraway, *When Species Meet*, p. 206.

53. The term 'transgenic' refers to 'organisms containing integrated copies of genes or gene constructs, derived from other species or not normally found in animals in their chromosomes. These so-called transgenes may or may not be expressed' (Maurizio Salvi, 'Transforming Animal Species: The Case of Oncomouse', *Science and Engineering Ethics*, 7, 2001, p. 16).

54. Rosemary Robins, 'Inventing Oncomice: Making Natural Animal, Research Tool and Invention Cohere', *Genomics, Society and Policy*, 4:2, 2008, p. 22.

55. Ibid., p. 29.

56. Ibid., p. 31.

57. Donna Haraway, *Modest_Witness@Second_Millenium.FemaleMan©_ Meets_OncoMouse™: Feminism and Technoscience* (New York: Routledge, 1997), p. 89.

58. Ibid., p. 55.

59. Ibid., p. 56.

60. Ibid., p. 60.

61. Ibid., p. 61.

62. Ibid.

63. Ibid., p. 66.

64. Ibid., p. 79.

65. Ibid., p. 82.

Epilogue: A Vicious Circle

In Jon Coleman's history of colonial America's relationship with its native wolves, *Vicious* (2004), he retells the tale of the death of a wolf named by hunters 'Old Whitey'. On the first telling, Old Whitey, on being caught in a snare, fought with such violence to escape the trap that the effort left him with patches of raw skin from torn-out fur and with bloody, broken teeth. The hunters took him alive, but the wolf, defiant, refused food and water, eventually dying of a 'broken heart' by the third day of his captivity.[1] On the second telling, Old Whitey is wrested from this romanticised and anthropomorphic reading of his behaviour:

> Whitey was terrified. The traps snapped and he panicked. He demolished foliage, shredded his coat, and cracked his teeth in wild fear. Following his capture, Whitey grew passive ... He advertised his submission, but the hunters wanted to dispatch a worthy foe rather than execute a cringing subordinate. They interpreted the gestures to fit their vision. They saw stoicism in the beast's passivity, not fear.[2]

Coleman notes that histories of this inter-specific relationship have tended to cast the two main players in the guise of either good or evil, both wolf and human equally befitting the role of fearsome predator depending on the stance of the narrator, but these histories have never quite captured the complexity of their interactions. Towards this goal of understanding such a long and complex relationship, Coleman's study centres on 'the violent interaction of three timeframes – historical, folkloric, and biological – [which] explains the longevity of wolf hatred and the brutality of wolf killing, as well as the rise of wolf popularity'.[3] For example, the very possibility of a second account of Whitey's capture has arisen in the development of the study of wolf behaviour, itself reflecting the growth in the biological and environmental scientific efforts to conserve rather than to conquer. This behavioural scientific account acknowledges the sophistication of lupine forms of communication, and the centrality of the formation and maintenance of social bonds:

> Wolves hunt, play, travel, establish pecking orders, create affective bonds, educate pups, demarcate territories, and converse in a language of howls, scents, and gestures. Wolves rarely attack humans, and they do not howl at the moon. (There is no record of a nonrabid wolf killing a human in North America since the arrival of Europeans.) They are neither innate cowards nor wanton killers.[4]

Coleman goes on to place American wolves and people on comparable trajectories, both aiming for increased territorial expansion. Wolves, he argues, employ a relatively simple and rigid form of communication, which only seems to reinforce the assumption that the flexibility of the sign characterising human language makes us their natural superiors. However, Coleman continues, 'like people, wolves colonized, and their unpretentious signals proved an effective aid to their adventures in territorial acquisition'.[5] Wolf territories are based on 'spacing' not space: their territorial behaviour signals others to keep their distance within a space that expands and contracts in line with the changes of season as much as the wanderings of the pack. All of this is alien to the basis of human territoriality in the ownership of fixed tracts of land and the treatment of the bodies of livestock as property.[6] Thus the conflict between humans and wolves is read as a clash of fundamentally different kinds of territoriality, and it is a deadly conflict that led to the decimation of the wolf population in the United States. Wolves preyed on domestic livestock, thereby incurring the wrath of landowners for the destruction of their property, and were hunted and even 'punished' for their incursions (tied up and hauled behind horses, or baited with meat spiked with mackerel hooks).[7]

The story of Old Whitey reveals the prejudices of colonial settlers at the time, and through the dual perspectives of hunters and biologists, separated by years of developments in 'expertise' on wolf behaviour, we see the interlocking influences of folklore and biology on attitudes towards wild animals. It is the later biological understanding of the wolf's behaviour that promises a future of greater tolerance of forms of territoriality that are completely other to our own property-based forms. In this respect, Coleman's study recalls Stephen Jay Gould's recounting of the story of Walcott's discovery and interpretation of the Burgess Shale fossils, for its culturally driven, distorted vision of evolutionary perfectionism. It also echoes Donna Haraway's dissection of the history of primatology, in which monkeys and apes have been treated as living depictions of our lost origins. Their behaviours, interpreted as

the prefiguration of our own, secured our senses of both their physiological and moral inferiority to human beings, and it was only efforts
to think animal life from the margins of human value and experience
that yielded constructive insights into the animals' behaviour.

Henri Bergson suggests, within a number of his works, a method for
overcoming philosophical dualisms, such as mind/body, possible/real,
and, implicitly, human/animal. Instead of trying to define each term of
the dualism as an isolated concept, we should consider them at their
points of intersection. Coleman's *Vicious* does precisely this in order
to understand the history of the human/wolf conflict, particularly in
the parallel readings of human and lupine forms of territoriality and
the role of communication in establishing and holding territories once
gained. I have suggested that the concept of pathological life can also
function as a means of thinking the human/animal distinction at its
points of convergence. At first, commonalities of human and animal life
arise in the rejection of a world-view based on the Great Chain of Being.
It is not that living beings exist in a plenum of lesser or greater states
of perfection, but rather that the process of evolution is replete with
false starts, errors, accidents and catastrophes. Pathology and error are
as significant in the formation of species as the 'creative' explosions of
life on this planet, and an acknowledgment of this displaces human
life from the top or end of any evolutionary chain. Furthermore, not
only is pathology – understood as divergence from a norm – integral to
evolution, it also comes to replace vital or creative force as the defining
feature of the living organism. This is at least true from the perspective
of medical perception aimed at the regulation and control of human
life, both at the level of the individual organism and at the level of
trends in human and animal population health.

While thinking life in terms of its relation to disease and death offers
novel and productive insights into its processes, the category of the
pathological carries within it the dual potential to either reinforce the
human/animal boundary in its hierarchical sense or to dissolve it. The
writings of Derrida, Levinas and Deleuze and Guattari each examine
the concept of animality as the indistinct fringe of endeavours that are
ordinarily thought to be distinctly human: politics, ethics and art. The
figure of the animal as outsider or anomaly often serves as a metaphor
or distorted mirror of human activity, reflecting back to us the reality
of our mistakes, ironies and limitations (perhaps akin to the revela-
tory and critical power of utopian and dystopian literature). However,
against this usage of animal metaphors and symbols, Derrida identifies
a particular challenge before us in his reflections on our failure to think
of animals as individuals, and on our responsibilities towards them.

Philosophical, literary and scientific inscriptions of animal life have all contributed to this failure to think animality, but, we have also seen, in the work of Donna Haraway, an exploration of the roles of companion species that continues a trajectory in Continental philosophy towards the dehumanisation (and indeed devitalisation) of human life. Haraway's combination of Whitehead and Derrida poses questions about our relationships with non-human animals on two levels: with Whitehead, we can start to think about the nature of the relation between ourselves and our environment at a pre-subjective level. It is not interactions between whole subjects that counts, but rather interactions between prehensions. If this is the basis of real interaction, then we can begin to reformulate what it is that constitutes our relationships with other animals. The microscopic analysis of prehensive relations means that I can engage in a reciprocal exchange of meaning, in a very real sense, with a cat. On the Derridean level, as it were, one can focus on the relations of mutual dependency and compassion at one end of the scale, up to breeding for food, experimentation, hunting and other forms of violence at the other. We have seen the complex array of factors at play in constructing animal life as mechanical or technical objects under the gaze of the life sciences and medicine, but there are also opportunities here, that the sciences afford us, to encounter animals outside of the dynamics of conflict and subordination. Interspecies relationships based on 'play' rather than utility, relationships that are as evident in human-animal interactions as those based on exploitation and violence, attest to the capacities of both humans and non-humans to initiate and form close bonds. From these reflections, it is clear that before we can even enter into ethical discussions about our attitudes towards and treatment of other animals, we must reconsider, very carefully, the persisting assumptions and prejudices about animals' lives and the shifting foundations upon which these lives are continually cast and recast as variously worthy of consideration and compassion, or incapable of reason, feeling or responsibility.

This is not to ignore some significant challenges that persist in our treatment of other animals. A key conflict exists between the ideals of the environmentalist movement (e.g. biocentrism) and those of the animal rights or advocacy movements. Discussions in the last chapter of this book raised the problem of the status of animals kept in captivity; whether of animal lives 'captured' through the slow process of domestication (kept as pets or used in laboratories) or of wild animals kept in zoos, circuses, or bred for the purposes of conservation. The very same difficulty that Derrida identified of viewing animals as species or kinds, as opposed to treating them as individuals, defines the boundary between the biocentric goal of preserving ecological networks and the animal advocate's concern for the suffering of a rat in a laboratory.

It is a difficulty that was also enacted in the 'escape' of a pack of five timber wolves from a zoo in the UK in November 2013.[8] Having happened upon a breach in the fence of their enclosure, and consistently with wolf behaviour, the 'pack' took an opportunity to explore and expand their territory (to 'disperse' is another characteristic of the wolf's territorial behaviour). The adventure ended with three wolves shot dead by police, in response to the uncertain threat they posed to the local human population. The eradication of the wild wolf population in England hundreds of years ago; the fundamental discord between territories marked by scent and sound and those marked by fences; and the human concept of ownership of land and animal bodies – all of these factors prefaced an inability to discern the effects of captivity on the animals and the recourse to an act of violence.

NOTES

1. Jon Coleman, *Vicious: Wolves and Men in America* (New Haven and London: Yale University Press, 2004), p. 213.
2. Ibid., p. 214.
3. Ibid., p. 4.
4. Ibid., p. 3.
5. Ibid., pp. 22–3.
6. Ibid., p. 24.
7. Ibid., p. 36.
8. Josh Halliday, 'Three timber wolves shot dead after an escape from Essex Zoo', *The Guardian*, 26 November 2013. Available at <http://www.theguardian.com/uk-news/2013/nov/26/wolves-escaped-shot-dead-colchester-zoo> (last accessed 3 December 2013).

Bibliography

Agamben, Giorgio, *The Open*, trans. Kevin Attell (Stanford: Stanford University Press, 2004).

Aminoff, Michael J., 'Brown-Séquard and His Work on the Spinal Cord', *Spine*, 21:1, 1996, pp. 133–40.

Ansell-Pearson, Keith, *Germinal Life: The Difference and Repetition of Deleuze* (London and New York: Routledge, 1999).

Ansell-Pearson, Keith, *Philosophy and the Adventure of the Virtual: Bergson and the Time of Life* (London and New York: Routledge, 2002).

Appel, Toby A., *The Cuvier-Geoffroy Debate: French Biology in the Decades Before Darwin* (Oxford: Oxford University Press, 1987).

Barthélemy-Madaule, Madeleine, *Lamarck the Mythical Precursor: A Study of the Relations Between Science and Ideology*, trans. M. H. Shank (Cambridge, MA: The MIT Press, 1982).

Bentham, Jeremy, *An Introduction to the Principles of Morals and Legislation, Volume 2* (Oxford: Clarendon Press, [1789] 1823).

Benveniste, R. E., R. Heinemann, G. L. Wilson, R. Callahan and G. J. Todaro, 'Detection of Baboon Type C Viral Sequences in Various Primate Tissues by Molecular Hybridization', *Journal of Virology*, 14:1, 1974, pp. 56–67.

Bergson, Henri, *Œuvres* (Paris: Presses Universitaires de France, 1959).

Bergson, Henri, *Mélanges* (Paris: Presses Universitaires de France, 1972).

Bergson, Henri, *Mind-Energy: Lectures and Essays*, trans. H. Wildon Carr (Westport, CT: Greenwood Press, 1975).

Bergson, Henri, *The Two Sources of Morality and Religion*, trans. R. Ashley Audra and Cloudesley Brereton (Indiana: University of Notre Dame Press, 1977).

Bergson, Henri, *Matter and Memory*, trans. N. M. Paul and W. S. Palmer (New York: Zone Books, 1991).

Bergson, Henri, *The Creative Mind: An Introduction to Metaphysics*, trans. Mabelle L. Andison (New York: Citadel Press, 1992).

Bergson, Henri, *Creative Evolution*, trans. Arthur Mitchell (New York: Dover, 1998).

Bergson, Henri, *Duration and Simultaneity*, trans. Leon Jacobson, ed. Robin Durie (London: Clinamen, 1999).

Bergson, Henri, *Time and Free Will: An Essay on the Immediate Data of Consciousness*, trans. F. L. Pogson (New York: Dover, 2001).

Bergson, Henri, *Key Writings*, ed. Keith Ansell-Pearson and John Mullarkey (London: Continuum, 2002).

Bergson, Henri, 'Psycho-physical Parallelism and Positive Metaphysics', in Gary Gutting (ed.), *Continental Philosophy of Science* (Oxford: Blackwell, 2005), pp. 59–68.

Bernard, Claude, *An Introduction to the Study of Experimental Medicine*, trans. Henry Copley Greene (New York: Dover, [1865] 1957).

Bichat, Xavier, *Physiological Researches on Life and Death*, trans. F. Gold, with notes by F. Magendie, trans. George Hayward, in Daniel N. Robinson (ed.), *Significant Contributions to the History of Psychology 1750–1920* (Washington DC: University Publications of America, [1800] 1978).

Birke, Lynda and Luciana Parisi, 'Animals, Becoming', in H. Peter Steeves (ed.), *Animal Others* (New York: SUNY Press, 1999), pp. 55–73.

Bisgould, Lesli, 'Power and Irony: One Tortured Cat and Many Twisted Angles to Our Moral Schizophrenia about Animals', in Jodey Castricano (ed.), *Animal Subjects: An Ethical Reader in a Posthuman World* (Waterloo: Wilfrid Laurier University Press, 2008), pp. 259–70.

Braidotti, Rosi, *Metamorphoses: Towards a Materialist Theory of Becoming* (Oxford: Blackwell, 2002).

Braidotti, Rosi, 'Posthuman, All Too Human: Towards a New Process Ontology', *Theory Culture Society*, 23, 2006, pp. 198–208.

Buchanan, Brett, *Onto-ethologies: The Animal Environments of Uexküll, Heidegger, Merleau-Ponty, and Deleuze* (New York: SUNY Press, 2008).

Calarco, Matthew, *Zoographies: The Question of the Animal from Heidegger to Derrida* (New York: Columbia University Press, 2008).

Canguilhem, Georges, *Ideology and Rationality in the Life Sciences*, trans. Arthur Goldhammer (Cambridge, MA: The MIT Press, 1988).

Canguilhem, Georges, *The Normal and the Pathological*, trans. Carolyn R. Fawcett (New York: Zone Books, 1991).

Canguilhem, Georges, *A Vital Rationalist: Selected Writings from Georges Canguilhem*, ed. Francois Delaporte (New York: Zone Books, 2000).

Canguilhem, Georges, 'Commentaire au troisième chapitre de *L'Évolution créatrice*', in Frédéric Worms (ed.), *Annales bergsoniennes III: Bergson et la science* (Paris: Presses Universitaires de France, 2007), pp. 113–60.

Canguilhem, Georges, *Knowledge of Life*, trans. Stefanos Geroulanos and Daniela Ginsburg (New York: Fordham University Press, 2008).

Coetzee, J.M., *Disgrace: A Novel* (Harmondsworth: Penguin Books, 1999).

Coetzee, J.M., *The Lives of Animals* (London: Profile Books, 2000).

Coleman, Jon, *Vicious: Wolves and Men in America* (New Haven and London: Yale University Press, 2004).

Conway Morris, Simon, *Life's Solution: Inevitable Humans in a Lonely Universe* (Cambridge: Cambridge University Press, 2003).

Cottingham, John, '"A Brute to the Brutes?": Descartes' Treatment of Animals', *Philosophy*, 53, 1978, pp. 551–9.

Cuvier, Georges, *The Animal Kingdom: Arranged According to its Organization*, trans. H. McMurtrie (London: Orr and Smith, 1834).

Darwin, Charles, *The Origin of Species* (Oxford: Oxford University Press, [1859] 1996).

Dawkins, Richard, *The Selfish Gene* (Oxford: Oxford University Press, 1976).

Dawkins, Richard, *The Extended Phenotype* (Oxford: Oxford University Press, 1982).

de Beauvoir, Simone, *The Second Sex*, trans. H. M. Parshley (London: Vintage, 1953).

de Fontenay, Elisabeth, *Le Silence des bêtes: La philosophie à l'épreuve de l'animalité* (Paris: Fayard, 1998).

de Fontenay, Elisabeth, *Without Offending Humans: A Critique of Animal Rights*, trans. Will Bishop (Minneapolis: Minnesota University Press, 2012).

Deleuze, Gilles, *Le Bergsonisme* (Paris: Presses Universitaires de France, 1966).

Deleuze, Gilles, *Bergsonism*, trans. Hugh Tomlinson and Barbara Habberjam (New York: Zone Books, 1991).

Deleuze, Gilles, and Félix Guattari, *A Thousand Plateaus*, trans. Brian Massumi (London: Athlone, 1982).

Derrida, Jacques, *Points: Interviews, 1974–1994*, ed. Elisabeth Weber (Stanford: Stanford University Press, 1995).

Derrida, Jacques, *The Animal That Therefore I Am*, trans. D. Wills (New York: Fordham University Press, 2008).

Dombrowski, Daniel A., *Hartshorne and the Metaphysics of Animal Rights* (New York: SUNY Press, 1988).

Donovan, Josephine, 'Feminism and the Treatment of Animals: From Care to Dialogue', in S. J. Armstrong and R. G. Botzler (eds), *The Animal Ethics Reader*, 2nd edn (London: Routledge, 2003), pp. 47–54.

Durie, Robin, 'Creativity and Life', *The Review of Metaphysics*, 56, December 2002, pp. 357–83.

During, Elie, 'A History of Problems: Bergson and the French Epistemological Tradition', *The Journal of the British Society for Phenomenology*, 35:1, January 2004, pp. 4–23.

Eimer, Gustave Heinrich Theodor, *Organic Evolution as the Result of the Inheritance of Acquired Characters According to the Laws of Organic Growth*, trans. J. T. Cunningham (London: Macmillan and Co., 1890).

Eimer, Gustave Heinrich Theodor, *On Orthogenesis and the Impotence of Natural Selection in Species-Formation*, trans. Thomas J. McCormack (Chicago: The Open Court Publishing Company, 1898).

Emmett, Dorothy, *The Nature of Metaphysical Thinking* (London: Macmillan, 1961).

Emmett, Dorothy, *Whitehead's Philosophy of Organism* (London: Macmillan, 1966).

Foucault, Michel, 'Polemics, Politics, and Problemizations: An Interview with Michel Foucault', in Paul Rabinow (ed.), *The Foucault Reader* (Harmondsworth: Penguin, 1984), pp. 381–90.

Foucault, Michel, *The Birth of the Clinic*, trans. A. M. Sheridan (London and New York: Routledge, 1989).

Foucault, Michel, *The Archaeology of Knowledge*, trans. A. M. Sheridan Smith (London and New York: Routledge, 1989).

Foucault, Michel, *The History of Sexuality, Volume 1: An Introduction*, trans. Robert Hurley (New York: Vintage Books, 1990).

Foucault, Michel, *The History of Sexuality, Volume 3: The Care of the Self*, trans. Robert Hurley (London: Penguin, 1990).

Foucault, Michel, *The History of Sexuality, Volume 2: The Use of Pleasure*, trans. Robert Hurley (London: Penguin, 1992).

Foucault, Michel, *Security, Territory, Population: Lectures at the Collège de France, 1977–1978*, ed. Michel Senellart, trans. Graham Burchell (London: Palgrave Macmillan, 2009).

Geoffroy Saint-Hilaire, Étienne, *Philosophie anatomique: Pièces osseuses des organes respiratoires* (Paris: J.-B. Baillière, 1818).

Geoffroy Saint-Hilaire, Étienne, *Principes de philosophie zoologique* (Paris: Pichon et Didier, 1830).

Goldstein, Kurt, *The Organism: A Holistic Approach to Biology Derived from Pathological Data in Man* (New York: Zone Books, 2000).

Goodwin, Brian, *How the Leopard Changed its Spots: The Evolution of Complexity* (New York: Charles Scribner's Sons, 1994).

Gould, Stephen Jay, *Wonderful Life: The Burgess Shale and the Nature of History* (London: Vintage, 2000).

Gould, Stephen Jay, *The Structure of Evolutionary Theory* (Cambridge, MA and London: The Belknap Press of Harvard University Press, 2002).

Grandin, Temple, *Thinking in Pictures: And Other Reports From my Life with Autism* (London: Bloomsbury, [1995] 2006).

Grandin, Temple, and Catherine Johnson, *Animals in Translation: The Woman Who Thinks Like a Cow* (London: Bloomsbury, 2006).

Greco, Monica, 'The Ambivalence of Error: "Scientific Ideology" in the History of the Life Sciences and Psychosomatic Medicine', *Social Science & Medicine*, 58, 2004, pp. 687–96.

Gunter, P. A. Y., 'Bergson and the War against Nature', in John Mullarkey (ed.), *The New Bergson* (Manchester: Manchester University Press, 1999), pp. 168–83.

Haeckel, Ernst, J. Arthur Thomson and August Weismann, *Evolution in Modern Thought* (New York: The Modern Library, 2007).

Haigh, Elizabeth, *Xavier Bichat and the Medical Theory of the Eighteenth Century* (London: Wellcome Institute for the History of Medicine, 1984).

Halliday, Josh, 'Three Timber Wolves Shot Dead After an Escape from Essex Zoo', *The Guardian*, 26 November 2013, <http://www.theguardian.com/uk-news/2013/nov/26/wolves-escaped-shot-dead-colchester-zoo> (last accessed 3 December 2013).

Haraway, Donna, *Primate Visions: Gender, Race, and Nature in the World of Modern Science* (New York: Routledge, 1989).

Haraway, Donna, *Simians, Cyborgs and Women: The Reinvention of Nature* (New York: Routledge, 1991).

Haraway, Donna, *Modest_Witness@Second_Millenium.FemaleMan©_Meets_OncoMouse™: Feminism and Technoscience* (New York: Routledge, 1997).

Haraway, Donna, *The Companion Species Manifesto: Dogs, People and Significant Otherness* (Chicago: Prickly Paradigm Press, 2003).

Haraway, Donna, *When Species Meet* (Minneapolis: University of Minnesota Press, 2008).

Harlow, Harry, 'The Nature of Love', *American Psychologist*, 13, 1958, pp. 573–685.

Hayles, N. Katherine, *How We Became Posthuman: Virtual Bodies in Cybernetics, Literature and Informatics* (Chicago: University of Chicago Press, 1999).

Heidegger, Martin, *Being and Time*, trans. John Macquarrie and Edward Robinson (Oxford: Blackwell, 1962).

Heidegger, Martin, *The Fundamental Concepts of Metaphysics*, trans. William McNeill and Nicholas Walker (Bloomington: Indiana University Press, 1995).

Henning, Brian, *The Ethics of Creativity: Beauty, Morality and Nature in a Processive Cosmos* (Pittsburgh: University of Pittsburgh Press, 2005).

Home Office, *Statistics of Scientific Procedures on Living Animals, Great Britain 2012* (London: The Stationery Office, 2013), <https://www.gov.uk/government/publications/statistics-of-scientific-procedures-on-living-animals-great-britain-2012> (last accessed 8 December 2013).

James, William, *Essays in Radical Empiricism* (Lincoln: University of Nebraska Press, [1912] 1996).

James, William, *A Pluralistic Universe* (Lincoln: University of Nebraska Press, [1909] 1997).

Jankélévitch, Vladimir, *Henri Bergson* (Paris: Presses Universitaires de France, 1959).

Jay, Martin, *Downcast Eyes: The Denigration of Vision in Twentieth-Century French Thought* (Berkeley: University of California Press, 1993).

Kant, Immanuel, *The Critique of Judgement*, trans. Werner S. Pluhar (Indianapolis: Hackett, 1987).

Kauffman, Stuart A., *The Origins of Order: Self-Organization and Selection in Evolution* (Oxford: Oxford University Press, 1993).

Kauffman, Stuart A., *At Home in the Universe: The Search for the Laws of Self-Organization and Complexity* (Oxford: Oxford University Press, 1995).

Kauffman, Stuart A., *Investigations* (Oxford: Oxford University Press, 2000).

Kauffman, Stuart A., *Reinventing the Sacred: A New View of Science, Reason, and Religion* (New York: Basic Books, 2008).

Kennedy, Emmet, 'Ideology from de Tracy to Marx', *Journal of the History of Ideas*, 40:3, 1979, pp. 353–68.

Kristeva, Julia, 'Women's Time', in Toril Moi (ed.), *The Kristeva Reader*, trans. Léon. S. Roudiez and Seán Hand (Oxford: Blackwell, 1986).

Levinas, Emmanuel, 'The Paradox of Morality: An Interview with Emmanuel Levinas', in Robert Bernasconi and David Wood (eds), *The Provocation of Levinas: Rethinking the Other* (London: Routledge, 1988).

Levinas, Emmanuel, *Difficult Freedom: Essays on Judaism*, trans. Seán Hand (Baltimore: Johns Hopkins University Press, 1990).

Levinas, Emmanuel, 'Is Ontology Fundamental?', in Adrian T. Peperzak, Simon Critchley and Robert Bernasconi (eds), *Basic Philosophical Writings* (Bloomington and Indianapolis: Indiana University Press, 1996).

Levinas, Emmanuel, 'The Name of a Dog, Or Natural Rights', in Peter Atterton and Matthew Calarco (eds), *Animal Philosophy: Essential Readings in Continental Thought* (London: Continuum, 2004).

Lovejoy, Arthur O., *The Great Chain of Being: A Study of the History of an Idea* (Cambridge, MA: Harvard University Press, [1936] 1964).

Luke, Brian, 'Taming Ourselves or Going Feral', in Carol Adams and Josephine Donovan (eds), *Animals and Women: Feminist Theoretical Perspectives* (Durham, NC: Duke University Press, 1995), pp. 290–319.

Merleau-Ponty, Maurice, *La Nature: Notes, Cours de Collège de France* (Paris: Seuil, 1994).

Merleau-Ponty, Maurice, *The Phenomenology of Perception*, trans. Colin Smith (London: Routledge, 2002).

Merleau-Ponty, Maurice, *Nature: Course Notes from the Collège de France*, trans. Robert Vallier (Evanston: Northwestern University Press, 2003).

Midgley, Mary, *Beast and Man* (London: Routledge, 1979).

Montgomery, Georgina M., 'Place, Practice and Primatology: Clarence Ray Carpenter, Primate Communication and the Development of Field Methodology, 1931–1945', *Journal of the History of Biology*, 38, 2005, pp. 495–533.

Moore, F. C. T., *Bergson: Thinking Backwards* (Cambridge: Cambridge University Press, 1996).

Mullarkey, John, *Bergson and Philosophy* (Edinburgh: Edinburgh University Press, 1999).

Oliver, Kelly, 'What Is Wrong with (Animal) Rights?', *The Journal of Speculative Philosophy*, 22:3, 2008, pp. 214–24.

Prigogine, Ilya, *From Being to Becoming: Time and Complexity in the Physical Sciences* (San Francisco: W. H. Freeman and Company, 1980).

Prigogine, Ilya, *The End of Certainty: Time, Chaos, and the New Laws of Nature* (New York: The Free Press, 1997).

Prigogine, Ilya, and Isabelle Stengers, *Order Out of Chaos: Man's New Dialogue with Nature* (London: Heinemann, 1984).

Ravaisson, Félix, *De l'Habitude; La Philosophie en France au XIX Siècle* (Paris: Librairie Arthème Fayard, 1984).

Ravaisson, Félix, *L'Art et les mystères grecs* (Paris: L'Herne, 1985).

Ravaisson, Félix, *Of Habit*, trans. Clare Carlisle and Mark Sinclair (London: Continuum, 2008).

Rees, Amanda, 'Anthropomorphism, Anthropocentrism, and Anecdote: Primatologists on Primatology', *Science, Technology & Human Values*, 26:2, 2001, pp. 227–47.

Regan, Tom, *The Case for Animal Rights* (London: Routledge, 1988).

Robins, Rosemary, 'Inventing Oncomice: Making Natural Animal, Research Tool and Invention Cohere', *Genomics, Society and Policy*, 4:2, 2008, pp. 21–35.

Rose, Nikolas, 'Medicine, History and the Present', in Colin Jones and Roy Porter (eds), *Reassessing Foucault: Power, Medicine and the Body* (London: Routledge, 1994), pp. 48–72.

Russell, Bertrand, *History of Western Philosophy* (Woking: George Allen & Unwin, 1946).

Said, Edward, *Orientalism* (London: Penguin, 2003).

Salvi, Maurizio, 'Transforming Animal Species: The Case of Oncomouse', *Science and Engineering Ethics*, 7, 2001, pp. 15–28.

Schiestl, Florian P., Rod Peakall, Jim G. Mant, Fernando Ibarra, Claudia Schulz, Stephan Franke, and Wittko Francke, 'The Chemistry of Sexual Deception in an Orchid-Wasp Pollination System', *Science*, 302, 17 October 2003, pp. 437–8.

Singer, Peter, *Animal Liberation*, 2nd edn (London: Pimlico, 1995).

Soulez, Philippe and Frédéric Worms, *Bergson: Biographie* (Paris: Presses Universitaires de France, 2002).

Stengers, Isabelle, *Penser Avec Whitehead: Une libre et sauvage création de concepts* (Paris: Seuil, 2002).

Stengers, Isabelle, *Cosmopolitics I*, trans., Robert Bononno (Minneapolis: University of Minnesota Press, 2010).

Stengers, Isabelle, *Thinking with Whitehead: A Free and Wild Creation of Concepts*, trans. Michael Chase (Cambridge, MA: Harvard University Press, 2011).

Stengers, Isabelle, *Cosmopolitics II*, trans., Robert Bononno (Minneapolis: University of Minnesota Press, 2011).

Tattersall, Robert, and Benjamin Turner, 'Brown-Séquard and his Syndrome', *Lancet*, 356 2000, pp. 61–3.

Thomas, Marion, 'Yerkes, Hamilton and the Experimental Study of the Ape Mind: From Evolutionary Psychiatry to Eugenic Politics', *Studies in History and Philosophy of Biological and Biomedical Sciences*, 37, 2006, pp. 273–94.

Twine, Richard, *Animals as Biotechnology: Ethics, Sustainability and Critical Animal Studies* (London: Earthscan, 2010).

Uexküll, Jakob von, 'A Stroll Through the Worlds of Animals and Men: A Picture Book of Invisible Worlds', in Claire H. Schiller (ed. and trans.), *Instinctive Behavior: The Development of a Modern Concept* (New York: International Universities Press, 1957), pp. 5–80.

Weil, Kari, *Thinking Animals: Why Animal Studies Now?* (New York: Columbia University Press, 2012).

Weismann, August, *On Germinal Selection as a Source of Definite Variation*, trans. Thomas J. McCormack, 2nd edn (Chicago: The Open Court Publishing Company, 1902).

Whitehead, Alfred North, *An Enquiry Concerning the Principles of Natural Knowledge*, 2nd edn (Cambridge: Cambridge University Press, 1925).

Whitehead, Alfred North, 'Mathematics and The Good', in *The Philosophy of Alfred North Whitehead*, ed. Paul Arthur Schilpp, 2nd edn (New York: Tudor Publishing Company, 1951), pp. 666–81.

Whitehead, Alfred North, *Science and the Modern World* (New York: The Free Press, [1925] 1967).

Whitehead, Alfred North, *Adventures of Ideas* (New York: The Free Press, [1933] 1967).

Whitehead, Alfred North, *Process and Reality: An Essay in Cosmology*, ed. David Ray Griffin and Donald W. Sherburne (New York: The Free Press, [1929] 1978).

Whitehead, Alfred North, *The Concept of Nature* (New York: Prometheus Books, [1920] 2004).

Wolfe, Cary, *What is Posthumanism?* (Minneapolis: University of Minnesota Press, 2010).

Wolfe, Cary, *Before the Law: Humans and Other Animals in a Biopolitical Frame* (Chicago: University of Chicago Press, 2013).

Wolsky, Maria de Issekutz and Alexander A. Wolsky, 'Bergson's Vitalism in the Light of Modern Biology', in Frederick Burwick and Paul Douglass (eds), *The Crisis in Modernism: Bergson and the Vitalist Controversy* (Cambridge: Cambridge University Press, 1992), pp. 153–70.

Worms, Frédéric, *Introduction à Matière et mémoire de Bergson* (Paris: Presses Universitaires de France, 1997).

Index